3.25/
AD

CX

THE
RECOVERY
OF
AMERICA

305- 1A- 2t

Books by John Charles Cooper
Published by The Westminster Press

The Recovery of America
A New Kind of Man
Religion in the Age of Aquarius
The Turn Right
The New Mentality
Radical Christianity and Its Sources
The Roots of the Radical Theology

NOV - 2 1973

Ce

THE
RECOVERY
OF
AMERICA

by
JOHN CHARLES COOPER

ANNEXE DE LA BIBLIOTHÈQUE
BIBLIOTHÈQUE
uOttawa
LIBRARY ANNEX

THE WESTMINSTER PRESS
PHILADELPHIA

Copyright © MCMLXXIII The Westminster Press

All rights reserved—no part of this book may be re-
produced in any form without permission in writing
from the publisher, except by a reviewer who
wishes to quote brief passages in connection with a
review in magazine or newspaper.

PUBLISHED BY THE WESTMINSTER PRESS
PHILADELPHIA, PENNSYLVANIA ®

PRINTED IN THE UNITED STATES OF AMERICA

Library of Congress Cataloging in Publication Data

Cooper, John Charles.
    The recovery of America.

    1.   United States–Social conditions–1960–
2.   United States–Moral conditions.   I.   Title.
HN65.C624   309.1′73′092   72-12533
ISBN 0-664-24967-1

To
My Comrades of the
7th Marines (Reinforced)
Korea, 1950
and
Especially to Those Who
Did Not Return

"In Us May They Find
That Fulfillment
They Forswore
In the Interest of Justice."

CONTENTS

PROLOGUE: WALKING DOWN THE ROAD

Bill Moyers has given us an insightful book called *Listening to America*.[1] John Steinbeck has written a beautiful story about a less agitated America in *Travels with Charley*.[2] The book that follows is also concerned with America. I would prefer to visualize my star-crossed love affair with the land of my birth as a walk down the road. America is preeminently a land of roads. Other countries have them, too. I have walked them, from North Korea to Austria to Finland, from Mexico to Japan to Canada. But the roads I remember most and know best are the roads of America. I have swung down the road with Negroes on the Sea Islands of the South, tramped through the snow on a road in western Pennsylvania, dashed through the rain along El Camino Real in California. I have climbed, puffing and struggling, up mountains in Washington State; strolled down Puerto Rican streets. Hitchhiking across this country is no strange experience to me. I hitchhiked to my wedding!

I have driven across this land, some 40,000 miles a year for fifteen years. I've ridden across it, sleeping disconsolately in the back of a Greyhound bus, riding thirty and more hours at a time. Riding and riding to get from graduate school to home on weekends. Sometimes while driving, riding, or hitchhiking I had to cry out, "Dear God, this country is so large!"

A big country, like a big man, can have a big fever. Nothing happens by halves in such a country. Much could be said about America, but nothing is said correctly that omits this base—the land, the fantastic bigness and variety of the land—and the wealth of human diversity in a population of nearly 210 million.

That sits heavily on my memory, too, as I presume to criticize America. Like the reader, I know and I've known all kinds of Americans. They are not a bad people. No one who knows Americans could maintain that. But like good people in Germany, Switzerland, or Russia, or anywhere, they sometimes do bad things, together and alone. The private sins of the Americans, and even their personal crimes, are their business. I don't want to dwell on these individual failings here, only on those failings which all of us as Americans, young and old, white and black, left and right, share. As a theologian, I am more concerned with corporate sins than individual failings.

Roads are important to this story of our collective problems, although they are not mentioned often as we go through the dreary drill of finding out what's gone wrong with America. Rather, the roads are implicit, they are the paper on which the book is printed, the unnoticed background that limits and fixes the story of an America waking up to look at itself after decades of dreamy sleep.

There is the road to Concord, with the Minutemen marching to make clear their independence. There is the road to Breed's Hill, where white man and black fought for freedom. There is the Wilderness Road, still hard to traverse, snaking through the aged wrinkles of the Appalachians out of Virginia, dropping straight down the mountainside into the hidden coves of Kentucky. There is Sherman's road leading to Chattanooga and on to Atlanta and through the burned crossroads down to Savannah and the sea and inland across South Carolina.

There is the road to Appomattox and the full roads, the muddy roads, full of disbanded soldiers and freed slaves with no place to go. There is the road, too, full of the bonus marchers of another war. And, on still another wartime road, stand soldiers under MacArthur, armed with bayonets and tear gas.

There was also a road that ran from Selma to Montgomery. I suppose I had every clerical collar I owned spread out along that road. Everyone wanted to wear a clerical collar that day. There was still a belief that being a clergyman was a protection against harm that day. Baptist and Brethren ministers don't usually have clerical collars; Lutherans do. I put up the collars. They were worn faithfully until a seminarian was kidnapped and killed and buried under a levee by the racists. Then those collars came off. Being a minister is no protection, these days, on American roads.

There is the road America followed to Vietnam. Bernard Fall has told the story of that road better than I can in his *Last Reflections on a War*.[3] That road started elsewhere, but it cuts across America, and it cuts deep. Men have marched along that road to the docks to disembark for southeast Asia. They have also marched on it to block the trains delivering war supplies. The road to, and from, Vietnam crosses the Columbia campus, cuts through Berkeley and Wisconsin. Twisting and turning, it cuts straight through hundreds of colleges and crosses a continental divide at Kent State University, in Ohio. That road has not yet been fully traveled. Its end must be reached.

There is the road that runs through the scalped hills of Pennsylvania and slices through the mountains of West Virginia. This is the road followed by the strip miners, the polluters, the spoilers. This road is littered with beer cans, candy wrappers, and, as in T. S. Eliot's epitaph for our civilization, "a thousand lost golf balls." Many times this road is made up of the superhighways we travel so much, the magnificent roads that carve the guts out of the more magnificent landscape.

The most dangerous road America now travels is the road of political polarization. That road has had a terrible casualty rate. John Kennedy was murdered as that road passed through Dallas; Robert Kennedy met his destiny as the road turned through California; Martin Luther King, Jr., was murdered as the road became a street filled with abandoned garbage trucks in Memphis, Tennessee. That road saw the deaths and woundings of twenty young students at Orangeburg, South Carolina; four students dead at Kent State in Ohio; more shot down at Jackson State in Mississippi. That polarization brought hundreds of thousands out into the roads and streets of Washington, D.C. More benignly, it brought hundreds of thousands to a few rural acres in upstate New York to celebrate as "Woodstock Nation," with its hymns to marijuana and its declarations of "Hell no, we won't go."

That road ran directly down Michigan Avenue and through the Loop on State Street in Chicago in summer, 1968. The promises of Richard Nixon, made in response to a sign carried by a young Ohio girl,[4] to "bring us together again" were never powerfully enough put into action to bring it off. We wait, stranded along the road of polarization, for the Government to run its course along the road from Vietnam, so we can move again toward the road of reconciliation. Narrow is the road (and steep) that leads to life; wide is the road that leads to destruction. I hope this book will move some of us toward the narrow road.

J. C. C.

Findlay, Ohio

INTRODUCTION

This book will attempt to assess the social and spiritual conditions current in the United States at the beginning of the eighth decade in the century of total war. It appears at a time when 1984 is chronologically only eleven years away. In terms of some developments, *1984* might be even closer. We wish to examine our culture in order to assess the real problems that have not been attacked and solved because of the overriding interest in foreign affairs, particularly in foreign wars, that has characterized this country since 1939.

This is not a book about the Vietnam War, although that war may still be going on, even if in a reduced way, when these words are read. It is a book written in the hope that the end of the Vietnam War will mark a close-out of American involvement that will allow us to turn our attention to the social sores that have been ignored during the last decade, a decade of Asian entanglement. We observe only the following facts as a point of departure for the studies undertaken here.

America has been involved in war in Indochina since the time of the Korean War. American involvement in the affairs of Vietnam, Laos, and Cambodia has siphoned off increasingly large amounts of American men, money, and material through the administrations of Truman, Eisenhower, Kennedy, Johnson, and Nixon. American prosperity, fueled in part by these war-related expenditures, continued to grow until 1970. Then the economic upswing stalled. Years before this economic illness appeared, the social problems of the neglected domestic scene burst like infected sores. The decades of neglect and oppression of blacks ushered in the civil rights movement. The limited success, legal but not actual, of this idealistic wave produced its own demise. The boils of Watts, Detroit, Washington, and Harlem broke.

The campuses, which had been misused on the one hand as baby-sitting facilities—their curricula serving as four-year "holding patterns" for an increasingly large group of "youth"—and which had been misused on the other hand for military research projects, to devise weapons and techniques of war, erupted at Berkeley, Columbia, Wisconsin, Michigan, and hundreds of other schools. With the growth of American physical involvement in Vietnam, expanding from a few thousands in 1961 to 550,000 by 1968, the campuses became centers of resistance to the war. The development of war resistance culminated in the killing of students at Kent State University in Ohio and Jackson State College in Mississippi (both in 1970) paralleling the killing of black students at Orangeburg, South Carolina, during the end of the civil rights struggle in 1968. Poverty, so often swept under the rug in America, became an issue precisely because so much wealth was being thrown away in an undeclared war and on the hardware to reach the moon in the "space race." Michael Harrington's research revealed that there is "another America" that includes those citizens who live at or below the poverty line. At the end of 1970 there were 25.5 million poor persons in the United States.[5] Despite "wars on poverty" and the reorganization of "welfare programs," the misery of self-perpetuating poverty continues. So does the waste of treasure in Vietnam,

Cambodia, and Laos, despite the phased withdrawal of American troops that has removed over five hundred thousand men from the combat zone since its high point of buildup.[6]

But the deeper sickness that has grown in America since the large-scale involvement of hundreds of thousands of men in Vietnam in 1964 has been the steady loss of faith in democratic ideals. The Government has sought to generate the national unity that usually prevails in times of crisis by deceptive reports both of dangers and results. Even worse, there has been a lack of honesty concerning goals and tactics. The revelations of the top-secret Pentagon Papers,[7] which were supplied to the newspapers by Daniel Ellsberg in June, 1971, only confirmed what millions of students and members of the counter culture already were sure of.

The prostitution of the university has proceeded as rapidly as the rape of the news media and the betrayal of the confidence of the people. The liberties of those still willing to think for themselves have been curtailed by a fantastic increase in the surveillance of thousands of individuals. The FBI and Armed Forces intelligence units have spied on and thereby intimidated many in public and private life.

The demoralization of the nation has been marked by the growth of drug abuse, which has been stimulated, not curtailed, by Draconian laws and their often unconstitutional enforcement. Tens of thousands of young men have been introduced to the drug habit by exposure to the very war they did not want. At first the connection between Vietnam and the growing drug problem was denied by the Government. But the evidence could not be silenced, and now the problem is admitted. This may be the first war in history to produce casualties from drugs as well as from combat and illnesses.[8]

These problems form the structure of American life as the Vietnam War seems to wind down for the United States of America. Of course, unless a totally new direction is taken in American life and in American domestic and foreign policy, we will not be free of the burden of Indochina for years to come. A new administration may signalize such a change, but, even if this fresh start is delayed, we will be freer to confront problems on the home front after active combat ceases. What those problems are and how they might be most suitably confronted is the topic of this book. America *after* Vietnam may be in as much danger as America *in* Vietnam. Certainly the problems we have put off facing squarely for so long are as complex as the jigsaw puzzle of Indochina, and they cannot be solved by mindless reliance on force or dissolved away by attempts at deception.

The truth may make us free, but only after the pharaoh and his wizards have been faced down, the Nile and the desert have been crossed, and the stone tablets of national priorities have been hewn out by human intelligence and human sweat. We shall not come and reason together if only words are used, nor shall we be brought together by empty television gestures. Only a hard look at the spiritual sickness that pits two cultures against each other in our country will lead us to reason. Only concern demonstrated in the sacrifice of privilege and in hard work on our rotting cities and polluted countryside, among our neglected people and alienated youth, can make us whole.

1

AMERICA'S IDENTITY CRISIS

America has lived as a nation with its head "under a bucket" for years because of the war in Asia. It could be said that this living in unreality was unconsciously desired by those in power, although those in power must be taken to mean members of all factions of every political party in the United States during the space of at least four administrations. It is not the intention of this book to make the case that one party or even one political philosophy has been guilty of neglect in America while the other party has found itself powerless to do anything constructive because of its lack of popular support. Both of the major political parties and most of the outstanding political leaders of our times have been involved in the prosecution of the Vietnam War. Criticism of the government on the point of misplaced priorities cuts both ways.

According to some psychoanalytical theories, those who do not complete a task at some stage of their psychological development are doomed to replay that problem over and over again until complete disintegration of personality occurs or until the task is completed by means of therapy or sudden insight in later life. I would suggest that America has suffered from a crisis of its identity and its development precisely because it has failed to solve the problems that arose at earlier stages of its life and has therefore suffered from recurring social stresses for over a century, stresses that were unnecessary as well as self-defeating.

The decade of the 1960's saw us awaken to the true causes of disharmony in America. The 1970's brought into sharp focus the unjust social order of this country, many people then recognizing that segregation and the attendant forms of discrimination visited upon the blacks, Mexican-Americans, and American Indians were not simply the product of a cultural lag between an advanced section of the country (the North), and a backward section of the country (the South). These dysfunctions were actually what should have been expected in a society that saw the problems of racism and exploitation only in their surface aspects.

The various movements toward social reform in America in the 1960's created a wave of fear in those who identified the *status quo* in race relations and wealth distribution with the practice of democracy. Each victory in the courts for an extension of civil rights had its counterproductive twin in the furnishing of another example of America's "drift toward socialism" for the propaganda leaders of the growing right wing. It is perhaps no accident that the leaders and heroes of the right wing, men such as Senator Strom Thurmond, were the outspoken advocates of the expansion of the war in Southeast Asia.

From the beginning of overt American military intervention in Indochina, leaders of the right wing in political office and industry saw the Asian war as a marvelous opportunity to rally the people of America around their favorite cause, anticommunism. Perhaps they felt that such involvement would take the public's eye off the real domestic problems and give an excuse to slow down social reform at home and divert federal expenditures to military projects that benefited their constituencies and magnified their own political power. Whether this was the result of cold-blooded planning or not, such was the effect of entering more heavily into the war after 1964. Is it an accident that senators and representatives who are the chief supporters of textile, oil, and munitions manufacturers are the greatest "hawks"?

Even in 1971, when a majority of people in America seemed to be fed up with the Vietnam War (according to most public opinion polls), the right wing remained relatively strong—strong enough for the Republican administration to base much of its domestic policy on a so-called "Southern strategy." That the right wing is weakening is shown by the realistic moves of President Nixon toward Communist China. The dramatic moves of Nixon's administration to fight inflation, however, seemed designed to give conservative big business the best break possible.

THE FALLACY OF A STATUS SOCIETY

Life is fragile. It must be preserved. It is tenuous and rare in the universe. Life can be brought to an end by madness as surely as by death. Although life can be choked by rigid barriers self-erected to preserve it from chaos, it can also be swallowed whole by the vacuum of things. Chaos and formlessness threaten it as profoundly as tyranny. Split from its unconscious depth, life is not worth living, since it has no meaning under such conditions. Lured into its own depths by schizophrenia or drug misuse, there to be lost in mystic rapture, it is not lived at all, since only the conscious edge of life can be aware of its own growth and passing. Its only guides are the art and literature thrown up as markers of the human spirit by the intercourse of the conscious and the unconscious mind. Apart from this unity of the mind of man there is neither life nor death, only nonbeing.

The social drive that seeks to maximize the meaning of

life and to preserve it in its fragility, protecting it from chaos on the one side and from its own overprotectiveness on the other, is the basic political fact of life that should be embraced. Today chaos and control are engaged in heated battle for the possession of man's soul. This battle forms the stuff of our culture and is the content and thematic motif of our art, music, literature, drama, and cinema. Looking at our cultural artifacts must convince us at once that Aristotle is right: Man is a political animal. Man does not and will not find his wholeness in solitude and the development of individuality only. Solitude and the development of self-awareness are the foundations of our humanity, but they are stages which themselves must be surpassed. Beyond the individual is the group, above the person is the community. To rest too long in individuality is to run the danger of madness.

If we are plagued by too many Deep Southerners who forget that the Union won the Civil War, we are more seriously plagued by students of American culture who forget that the Civil War took place and is the paradigmatic symbol of America as a nation. Peopled by diverse groups, America remains diverse under the homogenized blandness of its Howard Johnson–Holiday Inn civilization. One of the horrors of the technological future envisioned in *2001—A Space Odyssey* is the Hilton Hotel and other sanitized institutions of today planted in space. The shallowness of so much of our cultural life is but a reflection of the surface unity of standardized hotels, expressways, restaurants, and one major language. America is far more fragmented than recent analysts of our culture claim. People fall into many more categories than Consciousness I, II, and III.[9] Where do blacks and Chicanos fit in Charles Reich's categories? The individuality that permeates even the organization mentality keeps us apart quite as much as our pablum-like television series and sports events bring us together.

AMERICA—CONTINENT AND NATION

"America"—the very name strikes one as awe-inspiring. America—the name incongruously given to half the world by the whim of cartographers. America—a chain of mountains, massive plains, great lakes and inland oceans stretching over two hemispheres, from pole to pole. Citizens of the United States of America rarely stop to think that citizens of Canada are "Americans" too, as are Mexicans, Brazilians, and Peruvians. "Americans," however, in the context of wealth, prominence, and power in world affairs, are understood by citizens of all countries to be citizens of the United States. Only Canadians pointedly refer to the "United States" or to the "States." For good or ill, the paramount power in North and South America is the United States, and the United States shares preeminence in the world at large with that other culturally diverse nation, the Soviet Union. Hence, what "America" does, and more importantly, what America is, has great ramifications for the whole world. The myths and symbols by which nearly 210 million Americans understand themselves and their country are of more than parochial interest. The future safety of the world may depend upon the sanity and wholesomeness of these symbols.

THE INFLUENCE OF SYMBOLS

A nation is formed by the symbols that come into being among a people. A nation is what it is because of the contents of the conscious and unconscious minds of the millions of people who use and give credence to the symbols of that nation. Nonverbal symbols such as the concrete symbol of the flag, or verbal symbols such as that of "the chosen people" (with its psychological determinism) are not consciously created. Rather, symbols spring into existence in the historical dimension from the "collective unconscious" (as Jung would say) of the historical group that forms them. But just because symbols —and the myths made up of those symbols—represent such a deep level of reality, growing out of the unconscious itself, they are morally ambivalent.

In a sense, symbols are beyond good and evil, for they partake of that dimension of reality which lies below the moral imperative, beyond the choice between right and wrong. Morality is a matter of conscious choice: it denotes the ability to inhibit impulses, to check behavior. Symbols grow out of a portion of man that lies beyond the range of moral choices. For this reason symbols can break into the world of concrete reality with a demonic power (such as the destructiveness brought by the swastika) as well as coming to light with healing, saving power (as is shown in the cross). Most symbols, however, are mixtures of the selfish and the selfless, of the good and the evil, and consequently are dangerous to the unwary. The symbols of nationalism clearly fall into this ambivalent category. Much good has come out of their appearance in history, but, equally, much harm. The eagle bears the arrows of war and the branches of peace equally. No national symbol is purely good or purely evil.

Before we can free the spiritual energy of America to the end of dealing with the unmet challenges of our decade, we must come to grips with the myth of America. This myth has been explored by a number of scholars from various disciplines, and I have dealt with it at some length in *The Turn Right*,[10] so I will only briefly describe it here.

THE MYTH OF AMERICA

The facts: "America" is a made-up word of little historical validity, stemming as it does from the name of
Amerigo Vespucci, a map maker and geographer of the
late fifteenth century. Like the associated term "Indians,"
it was a historical accident, not to say a bit of misunder-
standing, that fastened the name upon the continents of
the "New World."

"America" was not even the possession of Europeans
(who have made themselves dominant here, except in
certain parts of Mexico, Haiti, and Guyana) by right of
first discovery. Anthropologists know that the wandering
tribes of Arctic Asia crossed into these regions 15,000 or
more years ago.[11] Long before Columbus in 1492, the
Norse Vikings came from Greenland to Newfoundland
and attempted to settle there. The researches and adventures of Thor Heyerdahl in the voyages of the reed ships
Ra and *Ra II* now seem to demonstrate that it is likely
that Central America was penetrated by the culture of
Egypt thousands of years ago.

Nor was America settled exclusively by Europeans who
drove back the native population by force, trade, guile,
and treaty. The black man, from Africa, arrived on the
Eastern shores early in the seventeenth century, and
the Chinese coolie was imported in large numbers to the
West Coast and far West in the nineteenth century. The
population that settled "America" was (and remains) a
mixed bag.

Nonetheless, the language, customs, religion (to the
extent that any of the settlers were religious) and legal
traditions of Northern Europe assumed hegemony over
"America." Gradually colonies were legally constituted by
the British parliament or by act of the British crown. To
the north, Canada (after France was excluded from

power with the assistance of the more southerly colonies) was formed into British provinces, and in what is now the United States thirteen colonies were established. To the west, Spain was in vague control; to the south, Spain was in true sovereignty over an older, more developed empire. Britain had won the Eastern seaboard, the West Indian Islands and the far North only by aggressive action against "Indian," Frenchman, Dane, Dutchman, and Swede.

Little by little all the characteristics of British cultural and political life arose in the colonies. The thirteen colonies were, except for purposes of defense from external enemies and for reasons of state, independent and viable political units. The Revolutionary War only signalized that fact.

The colonies were not, however, well-fitted parts of a single nation, nor were they to become one except through the process of a protracted war (1775–1783). Even after a peace had been concluded it took time to unify and make legally real a United States of America. The Articles of Confederation were not a sufficient basis for a federal union. Years passed before the British abandoned all their forts in the old Northwest.

Not even the Constitution, with its "Bill of Rights," made necessary by the fears and hesitations of the various legislatures over signing the Constitution, made the United States a fully united nation. The concept of states' rights and the idea of the reserved ability to secede from the Union continued to haunt the new nation. The Southern states were not the first to threaten secession (New Englanders were first), but the constitutional legalists of South Carolina were the first to secede.

The United States, or "America," as it vaingloriously called itself, was a creature of compromise, pluralistically based, and subject to the stresses and strains of competing regions (including the Western frontier region), that gradually fell apart. It took the first modern total war, a war that bled one region almost to economic and social death, to overcome the grand compromise and produce "one nation."

From 1600, when Britain began to expand into America, to 1776 there is almost as wide a span of time as there is from 1776 to the present. Before that, there was a gap of 108 years from Columbus' discovery to the beginnings of British expansion. It took only 85 years for the new nation to dissolve (1776–1861). It has been "one" for only 108 years since its bloody Iliad from Fort Sumter to Appomattox. Someone has said that America has been calling itself a "new nation" for hundreds of years. Our "youth" is our oldest tradition. And yet, "America" is a twice-born country, and it is just over a century into the great experiment of democratic, federalistic pluralism. Whether its experiment will succeed is still in doubt.

According to the myth, America is the land of the free and the home of the brave. I suppose it is all in how one defines freedom and bravery. The American Legion, the John Birch Society, and the Daughters of the American Revolution—along with the grade-school history books—assert that the most religious, law-abiding, and hardworking stock of Northern Europe sailed to this continent to find religious liberty and the opportunity to put their tremendous creative energy to work and to govern themselves.

In this manifestly destined plan the pioneers were aided to a small degree by the native population, but more often they were attacked by murderous savages whose customary method of warfare included the slaughter of women and children.[12] Later, when the sturdy colonists sought to assert their independence from the half-mad German-speaking British sovereign, he wickedly paid these murderers of the forest to attack the settlers. This is, of course, the echo of a historical truth.

Once free of England's sway by virtue of their sacrificial and united efforts on the field of battle, the Americans (as they now are known) set about establishing the weakest form of central government possible commensurate with the creation of a viable nation-state. In this new country the individual and his rights were regarded as supreme.

No mention is given in the myth of the three-fifths compromise by which slaveholding districts and states were given three-fifths of a vote for each slave—regardless of the legal definition of the slave as "property." No "Indian" was franchised, of course, nor was the greater part of the population, which owned no land and paid no taxes. The regulation of the franchise was, interestingly enough, left to the states.

The American Dream

According to the traditional rendition of American history, men and women motivated by the highest ideals migrated first to the Eastern seaboard and then pushed westward to civilize an empty land. The only barriers to their efforts, except the distance, mountains, and rivers, were a few Indians. These settlers tended to reproduce a kind of Northern European society on the seaboard and then duplicated the communities of Pennsylvania, Virginia, and Maryland over and over in the territories farther west.[13] Wherever the pioneers went they carried the church and school and established law and order. Everyone obtained his own land and attained a sense of community responsibility. There was freedom of speech and religion, and the opportunity to advance socially was open to all. Gradually the frontier was populated to the degree that cities and territories could be formed. The latter were quickly admitted to the union as states. Over the course of the period 1791–1912 the contiguous forty-eight states were created on the base of the original thirteen colonies.

While history is frank about the inescapable truth that a large part of the national territory was taken from Mexico by force, this aggression is justified in terms which suggest that the Mexicans did not use the territory anyhow. The history of the relations between the European settlers and the native Indians is usually told in terms of the savagery of the Indians and the need of the peaceful settlers to protect themselves against them. Only in the past decade has the true story of the relationship between the whites and the Indians begun to be told by researchers such as Dee Brown in *Bury My Heart at Wounded Knee*.[14]

Undoubtedly one of the most enlightened political measures ever taken by any nation was the decision of some of the original colonies such as New York, Virginia, North Carolina, and South Carolina to cede their western territories to the central government. According to the Northwest Territory Ordinance of July 13, 1787, the territories that lay west of the established original states stretching to the Mississippi River were to be opened for settlement and controlled by Congress, which was to encourage the population to form self-governing legislatures and apply for statehood as soon as possible. This was done not only in the old West but also in the new Southwest, the far Northwest, and on the Pacific Coast, until even Alaska and Hawaii moved from territorial to statehood status after the mid-twentieth century.

The unfortunate feature involved in this enlightened political action grew out of a decision of the British imperial government that was one of the precipitating factors in bringing about the American Revolution. The area from the Alleghenies to the Mississippi was heavily populated by hostile Indians who resisted the encroachment of the whites on their hunting lands. The British, in 1774, having no better answer to the massacre of the settlers who had crossed the Alleghenies, had passed the Quebec Act, which extended Canada's borders south to the Ohio River and closed the old West to white settlement. Once the American nation pushed into this region there could only be a war of annihilation waged against the Indians. Daniel Boone and his compatriots figured in the opening of this war after the Revolution. This war was not concluded until shortly before 1850; even the young Abraham Lincoln served in one of its episodes, the Blackhawk War.

According to the traditional view of America, the United States was predominantly rural, made up of farms and small towns. There was much truth in this. The first census, that of 1790, reported a population of just under 4 million, with only five cities having a population above 10,000—New York (which was a metropolis of 33,000), Philadelphia, Boston, Charleston, and Baltimore. Only New York and Philadelphia had above 20,000. What is not said is that over a half million Americans were slaves, of whom a great number were born in Africa. Over one quarter of the people in the United States in 1790 were black. There was no single white nation which contributed anything like this number of people. The majority of those of white blood were from Ireland, Scotland, England, and Germany.

The rural and isolationist social origins of the nineteenth-century American population largely determined the politics and social customs of the new nation. While the United States was, in statistical terms, a rural and small-town nation until the eve of World War I, at that point the balance moved decisively to a preponderance of urban population. Long before this time the cities had been developing and had grown to become the dominant facts of American economic and cultural life. By 1900 some 30 million or more, out of 75 million Americans, lived in urban areas—as contrasted with some 5 million urban citizens out of 35 million Americans in 1860. By 1920, 55 million Americans lived in cities and towns, out of a population of 105 million. In 1960, the urban population formed 69.9 percent of the total population of just under 180 million. By that time over 125 million people lived in urban areas, which included 130 cities of over 100 thousand people, 765 cities of over 25,000, and 5,445 towns of over 2,500 population. By 1970, the Bureau of the Census reported 150 cities with over 100 thousand population; 27.5 percent of the national population lived in these "great cities." Of the total population of 205 million, 53 percent lived within fifty miles of the East or West coasts.

Despite this growing trend of urbanization, the United States throughout the 1800's and into the 1930's remained largely shaped and controlled by rural values. The people who formed the cities (especially after the disabling acts designed to prevent the immigration of people from southern Europe and the Orient) did not come as fresh settlers in America but rather came from the farm and the smaller town. Some of their stories are well known— the migration of the "Okies" from the Southwest after the ruin of their farms by the twin plagues of economic depression and the great dust storms caused by the failure to observe ecological laws;[15] the movement of Negroes fleeing discrimination and lack of opportunity in the South for the industry of the northern cities; and the exodus of the poor whites of Appalachia crossing the Ohio River to Cincinnati, Columbus, Detroit, and Chicago. But the people who left the countryside to live in the cities carried with them the ideals of their rural heritage. These ideals and their accompanying customs originated in the experiences (and the popular interpretation of the experiences) of life in the small town and countryside in nineteenth-century America. The basis of this vision was the belief that America was a pioneer country and that the pioneers were absolutely independent, having carved out a nation with their own local resources without governmental help.

According to the rural tradition of our history, government in the earlier days had been far away. In this view the main function of government was to keep out foreign interference, fending off invasion from without. Other than providing a reasonable amount of internal regulation through civil and criminal law and the maintenance of highways, the government was charged chiefly with staying out of the way of private activity. This was the way the rural citizen wanted things. This was the way his pioneer ancestors had wanted things.

In this pattern of thought, the pioneers were seen to have formed their own laws and customs. When an outsider came into their midst, he either conformed to the customs of the community or he moved on, heading ever westward. (This is not just a part of American mythology but a reporting of fact.) Individuals who did not fit into the social pattern of the community were driven out. There was actual persecution along various lines—racial (of Negroes, Orientals, and Indians), religious (of Mormons, Utopian groups, Amish, and other sectarians), economic (of sheepherders by cattlemen, of small farmers by stockmen), and national (of Poles, Slovaks, Italians, and others). In a real way, even the settlers of white blood found little if any community freedom in the small towns to which they originally came. Those few families who have kept a record of their ancestors' adventures usually record a movement from Europe to one of the Eastern cities, on to Virginia or Maryland, on to western Pennsylvania or Kentucky, then on to Ohio, Illinois, or farther west. When the immigrant struck open territory or when he was able to combine with people of similar backgrounds as in the Mormon settlements in Utah or the Scandinavian communities of the upper Midwest, he stayed. In point of fact, the extreme ethnocentricity of many American communities preserved the languages of Europe as the language of the farm, home, and church well into the second decade of the twentieth century and beyond. There were Swedish and Danish Lutheran churches, Slovak and Polish Catholic churches. The fire under the melting pot was quite cool in the rural hinterland as well as in the larger Eastern cities with their Little Italys, their Chinatowns and Germantowns. The widespread use of the German language was stopped only by hostile feeling during World War I.

The person who wished to be truly free had to move on, usually farther west. As long as there was open land and the idea, if not the actuality, of a frontier, the conditions for attaining liberty for white people were quite good. Of course, the American Indian was excluded from this possibility as was the citizen of Mexican blood and the large majority of Negroes. But despite the lack of unity in America, the failure of equality for all, the basic rural mythology bequeathed by the nineteenth century to the twentieth was one of individualism. This was a gloss over actual historical differences with the patina of pure white Anglo-Saxon language and surnames and the belief that America had produced the ultimate in personal freedom for mankind.

For millions, there was truth to this myth. Considering the sociological development from 1783 to 1950, from the standpoint of utilitarian ethics, the greatest good for the greatest number may well have been attained. However, in the lesser number and the lesser good done to them are found the seeds of present-day American social distress. As Lincoln remarked concerning the bloodshed of the Civil War, it may well be that the conflict and dissatisfaction that plagues us may go on until every drop of blood unethically wrung from the unjustly treated and every dollar unjustly exacted from the mistreated has been repaid in kind.

SEEDS OF POLITICAL DESPAIR

The governmental philosophy of the United States was framed in its Constitution and in the several state constitutions in an ambiguous manner, so that it was capable of being understood as favoring class control (that is, control by men of property and position) or by a more broad-based democracy. The several state charters were by and large democratic except for restrictions on the franchise revolving around poll taxes and property taxes and by the exclusion of black slaves from political life.

Additionally, state constitutions were written in such a way that one side of the bicameral legislatures would be controlled by propertied interests. The senate was originally chosen by such state legislatures and was therefore controlled by the privileged class. The method of choosing the president and the vice-president, the only officials in the nation supposedly chosen by the whole populace, was distinctly antidemocratic and still is. The president was to be elected by slates of electors from the various states, and although the power has rarely been exercised, there is no constitutional safeguard that would prevent an elector from voting for anyone he pleased to put forward for president. Only party discipline has democra-

tized the electoral college, although recent social agita-
tion in Southern states has brought party discipline and
loyalty into question. It is perhaps not far-fetched to consider the issues surrounding an unpopular war that has
polarized the American public more than at any time
since 1860–1865 as also endangering the party control
over presidential electors. George Wallace counted on
party disloyalty in his country-wide presidential cam-
paigns.

The essence of the American democratic experiment
lies in the unwritten social covenant that the minority,
even when it represents over 49 percent of the voting
public, will accede to the take-over of the powers of government by the majority as established by legal balloting.
It is true that the American experiment has worked amazingly well, and even in cases where the popular vote has
been greater for the candidate who by the eccentricities
of the electoral system has not gotten the majority of the
electoral votes, the "minority" has peacefully and will-
ingly surrendered control of the country to the "majority"
party.

What must not be forgotten is that there was a time
when a large number of states, seeing the real possibility
of becoming a minority either in their party or in the
national political scene and thus having their professed
vital interests endangered, left the Union rather than
submit to majority rule. That time was 1860, and the
withdrawals led to the severe wounding of the nation
and four years of war. During the recent polarized condition of the American public, there was at least more than
an academic fear that something like the events of 1860
could happen again. Some years ago a rumor swept the
country that the administration in power would attempt
to prevent elections in 1972. Many more people believed
it than we would like to think.

Abraham Lincoln, speaking of the necessity for majority rule, had the following warning to give:

All profess to be content in the Union if all constitutional rights can be maintained. Is it true, then, that any right, plainly written in the Constitution, has been denied? I think not. Happily the human mind is so constituted that no party can reach to the audacity of doing this. Think, if you can, of a single instance in which a plainly written provision of the Constitution has ever been denied. If by the mere force of numbers a majority should deprive a minority of any clearly written constitutional right, it might, in a moral point of view, justify revolution—certainly it would if such a right were a vital one. But such is not our case. All the vital rights of minorities and of individuals are so plainly assured to them by affirmations and negations, guarantees and prohibitions, in the Constitution, that controversies never arise concerning them. But no organic law can ever be framed with a provision specifically applicable to every question which may occur in practical administration. No foresight can anticipate, nor any document of reasonable length contain, express provisions for all possible questions. Shall fugitives from labor be surrendered by national or by state authority? The Constitution does not expressly say. May Congress prohibit slavery in the territories? The Constitution does not expressly say. Must Congress protect slavery in the territories? The Constitution does not expressly say.

From questions of this class spring all our constitutional controversies, and we divide upon them into majorities and minorities. If the minority will not acquiesce, the majority must, or the government must cease. There is no other alternative, for continuing the government is acquiescence on one side or the other. If a minority in such case will secede rather than acquiesce, they make a precedent which in turn will divide and ruin them, for a minority of their own will secede from them whenever a majority refuses to be controlled by such minority. For instance, why may not any portion of a new confederacy a year or two hence arbitrarily secede again, precisely as portions of the present Union now claim to secede from it? All who cherish disunion sentiments are now being educated to the exact temper of doing this.[16]

According to a certain line of analysis gaining some currency in our day, it may well be that the democratic principle of majority rule is itself the fundamental ground of discrimination and the present class arrangements in American society. Whatever can sustain itself with "majority" (politically understood, not in any necessary numerical sense) approval is legal, right, and good. This was the case before 1865 in the South in regard to slavery, and throughout the country after 1880 in regard to Jim Crow legislation. Some philosophic balance, some guidelines of morals, some checks and balances on majority rule (in the "republican" tradition) must obviously be found and implemented by the consent of the majority itself. The principle enunciated in the World War I "conscientious objector" legislation may be a guide here. But much deeper than the legal sense, a theological/moral/philosophic basis in the implicit covenants of society (rather than in the rights of man) must be enunciated.[17]

THE "WOUNDED KNEE" OF OUR SOCIETY

A building may stand for centuries before it suddenly develops cracks that condemn it to fall into disrepair and ultimate destruction. Often these cracks stem from flaws that were part of the original construction. A man will work hard for a number of years and seem in the best of health, and then fall dead, his health undermined by a heart condition that was unexpected and unsuspected.

America as a nation shows signs of having such flaws and cracks, cracks that have a history dating back to the foundational period before the birth of the republic. America may have such an unsuspected heart disease. America has been ill before; America suffered a severe stroke in early adulthood and shows signs of an approaching, more deadly attack of the same disease.

The flaw, the fatal disease, seems to be a misappropriation of the facts of American history stemming from the unquestioned white supremacy that was the creative force behind the expansion of European peoples into Africa and Asia and then on into America. Connected with this is the residual belief that only white Europeans contributed anything of importance to the creation of the New World. The American call for equality and independence was not originally seen as applying to nonwhites. It was applied neither to the one person in four who was black in 1789, nor to the Indians, as they were called, who had lived peacefully with white settlers in the southern and middle states.

This blindness to the presence of nonwhites in the body politic prepared the booby-trap of smoldering minority resentment that was a major factor in the Civil War and a chief factor in the second American (social) revolution that dawned in the 1960's.

Blindness to the humanity of racial and ethnic minorities also strengthened the age-old white conception that men of other races were less than human and could therefore be killed with impunity or trapped and sold into slavery. The nations and people of Europe were deeply guilty of the same attitudes and behavior as their American cousins, slaughtering North Africans and black Africans in the name of empire and money. For a long time Americans deluded themselves into believing that they did not participate in such aggressive imperialism. Perhaps no nation, including Russia under the czars, who expanded their empire to the Middle East and through

Siberia as far as Alaska, ever engaged in such treacherous dealings with a less developed race as did Americans with regard to the Indians and the Africans. Surely, for a nation that is not yet two hundred years old, it should be a cause for some shame that for eighty-seven of those years human slavery not only was legal but was considered the economic basis of over a third of the national territory.

The aggressive elimination of the native Indians was covered with the big lie of "the Indian wars." That there were few if any real wars is now a matter of public record. But it is still so inadequately known more than eighty years after the "final solution" that books simply reporting the facts now reach the *New York Times* bestseller lists. When one reads of the government plans to eliminate the Indians in the same manner that a farmer might eliminate animal pests, one cannot but be reminded of similar exposés about civilian massacres in Vietnam—also involving people of another race.

The apparent inability of much of the white population to consider other ethnic groups as human beings still lies at the root of the national problem with blacks, Chicanos, and Indians. This inability has been fostered by public education and the mass media in the form of romantic adventures of American settlement. It is more than just an amusing thing that the average Western movie showed Indians killed in great numbers. Every child has seen over and over again the Indian falling off his pony in dozens of movies. Somehow the Indian is not real. In the mindless movies made in and about World War II a similar unreality attaches to the mass slaughter of hundreds of Japanese. The chilling factor is that Wounded Knee and Sand Creek really happened to actual human beings in America, and that of many thousands of Japanese on Tarawa and Iwo Jima only a small handful, usually badly wounded, were taken prisoner. Indians and Japanese were "lesser breeds" to be fully exterminated in the most efficient, inhumane ways. In the Declaration of Independence, the American settlers complained that the English sovereign had turned the wild tribes of frontier Indians against the revolutionaries, saying that the known manner of warfare of the Indian was to slaughter man, woman, and child. Apparently, if that were the case, it was also true of the Americans, and current events suggest it may still be true. Some writers have suggested that the Indians learned about "scalping" from the whites who set out to exterminate them. That may be precisely what happened.

The Melting Pot Myth and the Pluralistic Reality

The moral blindness of the white American to the real humanity of the Indian, the black, the Mexican, and the Chinese (in the far West) made possible the growth of the "melting pot" myth. According to this conception, people from all over the earth came to the United States out of the desire to achieve liberty, contributed the richness of their various backgrounds to the whole and melted into a homogenous population with a common dedication to American law and customs. The public schools, teachers colleges, night schools, civic organizations, newspapers and magazines oriented toward middle-class business, and the periodic raising of mass armed forces all contributed to the growth of this myth and to its partial reality. But it was never anything but a myth.

America, except for a part of the population, has never been and is not now a melting pot. The various nationalistic communities in the large cities, complete with their own languages, stand as the proof that everything foreign did not melt. The existence of the unabsorbed 11 percent of the citizenry who are black or partially black tells us the myth is a lie. The abrasive and uneasy coexistence of Puerto Rican enclaves in our cities shows us that this is no melting pot. The difficulties experienced by the Chicano communities stretching from Texas to California to Michigan point to the same conclusion. If we consider the Indian reservations and the Chinatowns in America, the absurdity of the melting pot idea is even clearer.

This is the real crux of the American social trauma after the middle of the twentieth century: the system was able to absorb (with difficulty) those immigrants of white blood who differed from the Northern European norm only if they—and their children—were willing to become "galvanized" Anglo-Saxons. The system—both because of the tragic history of American colonization and because of white blindness to the real humanity of non-Europeans, strengthened by ignorance and prejudice that was actually taught as part of the Christian faith— was unable to deal with those who deviated from the white, Northern European norm. America has been, and is, more an empire embracing huge tracts of land and diverse peoples than it is one country. The rhetoric of the black revolutionaries who speak of the existence of colonies within America and claim kinship with the former colonial peoples of the Third World is not far from the mark. As hard as it may be to accept, this is the truth: until the white majority faces up to the realities of American history and of the troubled present, we will not find our way forward to eventual solutions to the social illnesses that are killing our country. The truth can make one free only when it is acknowledged, accepted, understood, and, most of all, felt, deep in the spiritual bowels.

2

THE DARK SIDE OF AMERICAN POWER

The myth of America did damage enough when it was responsible for mistreatment of the Negro, the Mexican-American, and the American Indian within the country. However, it has done far more damage to the country and to the world since it has been let loose on the rest of the world through America's worldwide commercial and military power.

One of the most pervasive elements of the American myth has been the declaration that the United States has not interfered and does not interfere in the affairs of other countries; that it has spent its history down to the days before and after World War II seeking to mind its own affairs, keeping to the letter of George Washington's injunction that we should avoid all entangling alliances. This, however, is not what history records. From the beginning we note that the United States has been prevented only by weakness from interfering in as many foreign affairs as seemed to be in the national self-interest.

One of the first acts of the American revolutionaries was to invade Canada, where they would have remained had they not been beaten at Quebec and Lundy's Lane. We have already mentioned the designs of the original Eastern seaboard colonies on the Western territories, land that was ceded to the United States by Great Britain

in 1783. The Americans expanded this territory by pressure on Spain until they got clear title to most of Ala-
bama and Mississippi from Spain in 1795. In 1803, America had acquired from France the Louisiana Purchase,
which more than doubled the size of the country. By
treaty, in 1818, the northern border of the new purchase
was fixed with Canada and the United States gave up a
small portion of the purchase for a larger portion of what
is now North Dakota and Minnesota. The dispute over
Maine's northern boundaries was settled with Britain in
1842, and 7,000 square miles of disputed territory in
northern Maine became American property. This settlement, the Webster-Ashburton Treaty, actually gained for
the United States Fort Montgomery, north of Lake
Champlain, as well, although it was built on Canadian
territory. The same treaty settled the northern Minnesota
boundary as well. By 1819, Spain had ceded eastern and
western Florida to the American flag. Already in 1819 the
southern portion of Louisiana had been recovered from
Spanish claim, and not long after this Americans pressed
into Texas. The Texan war erupted and, in 1845, Texas,
most of New Mexico, Colorado, and parts of several
other present-day states were brought into the Union. In
1846, the American claims to the Northwest, in what is
now Washington and Oregon and Idaho (to which the
United States had genuine claims), were upheld and the
northern border was fixed at the forty-ninth parallel, running fully across the continent.

By this time there was trouble with Mexico, perhaps
brought about by American colonization of California,
and that great southwestern chunk of the present United
States, including California, Nevada, Utah, Arizona, and
parts of other states, now was wrested from Mexican
control. Even this vast empire did not seem enough, for it
was found that the best railroad route south to California

ran through Mexican territory, so the Gadsden Purchase was made in 1853, adding territory to Arizona and New Mexico.

Not to be outdone, after the warlike interference in Mexican affairs that had so greatly expanded the country, Secretary of State William H. Seward brought about the purchase of Alaska from Russia (which wanted to get rid of it) in 1867. Already Seward had signed a number of advantageous treaties with China and had used diplomacy backed up by the might of the victorious Union Army to force France to drop its support of the adventurer Maximilian. In 1871, the United States won its further claims against the British over the question as to whether the forty-ninth parallel was to be extended to the middle of the Strait of Georgia between the mainland and Vancouver Island. Thus the San Juan Islands off the State of Washington, over which the United States and Britain once almost went to war because an American farmer shot a British farmer's pig, became American territory.

There was a slight pause between 1871 and the late 1890's while the land of the free noninterventionists digested the Indians. This was the period of the last Indian wars. These were not so much wars as they were illegal police actions undertaken against human beings who had been guaranteed the right to live on certain lands free of harassment by the whites. During the Civil War, settlement and exploitation of the West went on as usual, but without as much protection by the army because of the emergency. In the inevitable collisions between the whites who did not respect treaties and the angrier and angrier Indians, white casualties were suffered. The Federal Government instituted the policy of paroling captured Confederate soldiers who would go to the West to fight the Indians under Federal officers.

In 1867 the so-called Peace Commission Act was designed to clean up the Indian problem now that the Government had both hands free to deal with it. The Indians had already been displaced and put in danger of starvation in many areas by the mass slaughter of the American buffalo, or bison, herds. In fact, for the purposes of feeding the railway construction crews and for the useful hides, the buffalo was almost exterminated. The way of life of the Plains Indians was destroyed. They had followed the millions of buffalo up and down their migration routes and had drawn food, shelter, and clothing from these herds (even the fuel for their fires was buffalo dung). Now their territory was overrun by the railway and their livelihood was gone. Few human beings, if any, would not have fought back. Now they were to be gathered up into reservations, which were simply concentration camps of larger size than the later World War II variety. Their lands were given to the railroads as rewards for the construction of this necessity of American nationalism. The Government gave and lent huge sums of money to the railroads. Between 1862 and 1872, it granted 33 million acres of land to their companies. In all, between 1850 and 1871, Congress deeded almost 155 million acres of land that had originally belonged to the Indians to the railroad companies for this service. We need to remember that until 1867 no thought was given to moving the Plains Indians to the great reservations established in the Indian Territory (the present state of Oklahoma) and that until 1871 the Indians were dealt with as citizens of foreign nations, by treaty. After 1871 the farce of pretending to honor the ancient independence of the Indians was dropped and they were treated as wards of the state.

The Indians had no chance. What is more, given the myth of America, American white superiority, and the fact that the Indians held few press conferences while the Army had many, the Indians came off as the villains of the episode. This bit of fictionalized history formed the background of the Western movies that most of us grew up on, although from time to time the injustice of the white man and the mistreatment of the Indians came through, even in the Hollywood potboilers.

THE FINAL SOLUTION

The Indians fought back—Cochise in the 1870's, the Sioux in the late 1870's. In 1876, the Sioux inflicted their one tragic act of revenge on their enemies when, in June, General Custer and 284 men of the Seventh Cavalry were destroyed by chiefs like Crazy Horse, Two Moon, and Red Horse. Sitting Bull came out of this as the Indian hero. But this was not to be the last act. The Indians responded to a kind of messianic religion put forward around 1890 by a warrior from the Paiute tribe of Nevada, Wovoka, who taught them the Ghost Dance, which promised that the Great Spirit himself would wipe away the white man and give the earth back to the human beings who knew how to live with nature without destroying it. Wovoka, himself influenced by Western thought, saw himself as standing in the line of Jesus Christ.

The Ghost Dance spread among the Plains Indians and to the north through disciples of Wovoka. Sitting Bull's tribe in the Dakotas learned of the new faith about the time that their large reservation was taken from them and they were confined to six smaller areas (1889). The Sioux had not gone to war, although the Government had ignored a treaty made with them as recently as 1868 and had stolen nine million acres of land to open to white settlers. Now the Ghost Dance was with them, the Indian agents feared it, and the Army tried through its Indian police to arrest Sitting Bull. Sitting Bull was killed in this affair and the stage was set in the last months of 1890 for the final solution of the Indian problem.

The end came on December 29, 1890, at a camping spot on a creek called Wounded Knee. Already the heart had been cut from the body of the war chief, Crazy Horse, and buried near this stream. For those who believed in the religion of the Ghost Dance, Crazy Horse and all the other dead would soon rise again when the wilderness Messiah came into his kingdom and God made a new heaven and a new earth where the Indians could live in peace. The chief called Big Foot was leading his people to a place of safety when he was arrested by the Seventh Cavalry and taken to camp near Wounded Knee. Chief Big Foot was not sent to a military prison. That would have been bad enough. Instead, another Sand Creek type of massacre took place. The soldiers began firing into the band of Indians when a few of them objected to giving up their arms. Whereas the Sand Creek massacre in Colorado had left 133 Indians dead, this time approximately 300 Indians were slaughtered.

The Indian wars were over. There were not enough males left to carry on the fight. The surviving Indians were herded together on reservations, located on lands considered of least value to the whites. God or history was to have the last laugh, for just as the dark and forbidding Black Hills of the Dakotas given to the Indians by treaty in 1868 were discovered to contain gold, the Indian territory in Oklahoma and reservations elsewhere proved to contain oil. However, by the time this recompense came to light we were well into the twentieth century and it was too late to force the Indians off their lands.

EXTERNAL EXPANSION

The United States had expanded itself by pushing outward into lands that belonged to others weaker in power but that adjoined American territory. That the only barrier to American imperialism was greater force is proven by the raids on Mexico that were never tried on Canada after the opening years of the Revolution. The United States would stand up to Great Britain when necessary, as it did in the Revolution and in the unfortunate War of 1812 (when the Americans decisively defeated the British at New Orleans in 1815 after the treaty of peace had been signed and the battle could no longer affect the outcome of the war). But aside from these collisions, problems with England were settled by treaty. In 1798, the Americans even dared to engage in an undeclared war with the French, who were far away and without a great navy, but for the most part their targets were picked with care.

We have mentioned that in 1867 Russia was interested in selling Alaska, and although Congress could see little benefit in buying it, the expansionist sentiment was such that Seward was able to get the purchase price of $7,200,000. After the period of the Indian wars attention was turned to the Caribbean area, where the last of Spain's colonial possessions were located. Cuba had been attempting to overthrow Spanish government for a long time. Since 1850 the United States had been promoting its influence in Latin America. In 1890, a Pan-American Congress was held. The Secretary of State at that time, James Blaine, had already asserted American influence in South America to settle a war between Chile and Peru. Blaine asserted American power elsewhere, for example, claiming all the seals of the Bering Sea for the United

States. This claim was not allowed by the international arbitrators. In 1889, America looked beyond Latin America to the far Southern Pacific, to Samoa, where, along with Germany and Britain, it took control of those strategic islands. Ten years later, the islands were divided and the United States acquired the naval harbor of Pago-Pago.

In 1898, the United States assumed outright sovereignty over the Hawaiian Islands, which had long been controlled by American missionaries and their descendants, who commercially ruled the islands. Grover Cleveland tried to stop the annexation because it was clear that American nationals on the island had engineered a coup against the hereditary kingship, but he was overruled by Congress, and on July 7, 1848, Hawaii became an American territory.

Cleveland tried to slow down American imperialism in the Hawaiian instance but not in Latin America. Through his Secretary of State, Richard Olney, Cleveland stressed the Monroe Doctrine in the sharpest tones to Great Britain, which had a dispute with Venezuela over the boundary of British Guiana. Olney declared that, at the time (1895), the United States was practically sovereign in the Americas and that its fiat was law in the Western Hemisphere.

American expansionism became imperialism in the widest sense in 1898. Declaring war on Spain with the express intent of freeing Cuba, the United States defeated Spain in Cuba, Puerto Rico, and the Philippine Islands. The treaty of peace ceded Puerto Rico and Guam outright to the United States, gave it a protectorate over Cuba and an option on the Philippines. The original protocol of August 12, 1898, left the disposition of the Philippines to a treaty of peace, giving the United States control only of Manila Bay (Article III). In the treaty of peace signed December 10, 1898, Spain ceded the Philippines to the United States for the sum of twenty million dollars. This payment shows that the United States did not gain title to the islands by conquest only, but did use the defeat of Spain to force an exchange of control from Spain to America (Article III). The inhabitants of the Philippines did not automatically become citizens of the United States as had been the case in the acquiring of land from Mexico, France, Spain, and Russia. Rather, Article IX of the treaty declared that the civil rights and political status of the natives of the territories acquired (the Philippines, Guam, and Puerto Rico) would be determined by Congress. In words taken from the title of a popular book containing speeches by William Jennings Bryan and others, the Philippine question asked America what it wanted—"Republic or Empire?"[18] Congress answered, "Empire," although the mass media covered up the sound with tunes of glory.

Our history books place little emphasis upon the fact that as soon as the United States assumed direct control over the Philippines, an insurrection broke out led by the former leader of the guerrillas against Spain, Emilio Aguinaldo. From February 4, 1899, until the spring of 1902 a bitter war raged in which the United States brutally sought to put down the Filipinos. In effect this war was longer by many times and more costly in lives and money than the Spanish-American War itself. The forty-five caliber pistol, the riot gun and other standard army weapons were developed and introduced because of Philippine combat experiences. As was to be the case with the Vietnam War later, this war severely split the country, and not only opposition Democrats but Republicans as well charged the Government with imperialism.

In the early days of the twentieth century the United States continued to throw its weight around in the world, secure in the knowledge that not even the mighty British Empire with its great fleets could hope to survive a war with the United States. With a two-ocean navy, and without the drawback of being vulnerable in its homeland as Britain was, the United States alone was a match for the British Empire. Many of those who opposed taking over the Philippines claimed that the British desired the United States to have the Philippines precisely because entry into the field of imperialism in the Orient would make the United States more dependent upon the friendship of Britain for the protection of its overseas possessions. Considering the close ties developing between Britain and America and the desire of both nations to have open ports in China, these critics may have been right.

The United States also spread out across the Pacific Ocean beyond Hawaii making claim to a number of islands over a considerable period of time. Many of these islands were first claimed by merchant shipping from New England in the days of whaling expeditions and later by commercial interests who wished uninhabited islands for the collection of bird droppings, or guano, which was used for fertilizer and the preparation of chemicals.[19] A number of islands in the Line Islands were either annexed by the United States, jointly claimed with Britain, or taken over by Britain with United States claims. In the case of Canton and Enderbury islands, Britain and the United States established a condominium. The United States laid claim also to the Tokelau Islands, the Cook Islands, the Phoenix Islands, and others controlled by New Zealand and Great Britain. Meanwhile Wake, Midway, and Johnston islands were taken over. America was a Pacific power long before it defeated Japan and took over the Japanese mandate in the Mariana, Marshall, Palau and Caroline islands (1945).

The United Nations placed these island groups under the administration of the United States as a United Nations trust territory.

The above summary of American expansionism does not even include the shady international dealings with Colombia that eventuated in the creation of the country of Panama, or the building of the Panama Canal in Panamanian territory which passed under complete United States control. We have not mentioned the acquiring of the Virgin Islands from Denmark for twenty-five million dollars. These examples show that the United States, long before World War II, was not a peaceful country concerned with its own affairs. The affairs of the Americans have always included the affairs of others, just as is the case in the history of every country.

I do not mean to imply that America has been an imperial power of greater energy than other countries. Obviously Great Britain started earlier and did a more thorough job, as did France. Coming late on the scene, Germany and Belgium also sought and found empires. The Portuguese and the Dutch were in the imperialism business before the creation of colonies in America was undertaken by the British. Indeed, these two smaller countries, which in modern times have been close associates of the British Empire, have retained many of their overseas possessions. In fact, Spain, even after being thrown out of the Western Hemisphere and the Pacific Ocean, first by revolutionaries in South and Central America and then by the United States, retained many colonies on the coast of Africa as well as islands in the African region.

America is certainly not worse than any of these European countries, which sought overseas possessions, not worse than European powers such as Austria and Russia, which sought empires in Europe or in Asia. In terms of sheer expansionism, the conquest of Siberia, of the Asian regions north of the Middle East, and of the Oriental areas north and east of China by Czarist Russia probably outstripped the exploits of most other imperialistic powers. The point is this: For the most part, other countries have not had recourse to a myth which held that they were not imperialistic and expansionistic. Or, if they invoked such a myth, and to the degree that they invoked it, they were not believed by their own people. In the United States, however, generations have grown up believing that the United States is not like the other nations, is not imperialistic or expansionistic. Therefore we have come into the problems of involvement in world affairs in the last few decades without a consciousness of our own history as a nation that is understood by our people. This has made it almost impossible for us to respond adequately to the troubles we have gotten into in Latin America and Southeast Asia.

The Fatal Power of Myths

The African writer C. L. R. James, speaking of the fatal power of the British myth of progressive colonialism, which holds that the British have ruled people for their own good in order to bring them to self-government, declared that we do not live in a time when myths are dead but rather in a time when the creation of myths is more prevalent than ever before. James declared that the British were unable to give up their myth.

> They have made adaptations; they have discarded some elements of the myth and have added others. They have given up positions that they could not hold, as the Greek myths were continually organized and reorganized to suit new situations, but the myth itself remains.[20]

We had better hope that the United States is able to break through the cobwebs of its mythology, for it is this barrier to clear insight, and not any iron chain of military necessity, that binds us to militarism at home and abroad.

There are a number of other living myths in our day. There is the myth of *revolutionary Marxism*. This myth holds that history is determined by the inexorable forces of economics and that class struggle is inevitable in every society as it advances to the industrial stage. The outcome of this struggle is also determined by these forces. The proletariat—those who are disciplined to operate the factories, or, in the Latin American, Asian, and African varieties of this myth, those who operate the farms— must and will be victorious over the classes who own the factories and farms.

There is the myth of the *exploited colonial peoples*, which forms a separate myth in itself, although it is often mixed with Marxism. This myth has been examined by commentators such as C. L. R. James[21] and Frantz Fanon,[22] who tell us that it has been fashioned as the negative mirror image of the centuries-old myth of *colonial imperialism*. This myth sees the people of the former colonial territories, together with the members of minority groups within established countries, as suddenly having been raised to a level of consciousness where they see that their humanity has been denied them by those who rule them without their consent. In this rise to a new level of consciousness, the oppressed person sees himself as incomplete—in psychoanalytical terms, as not having a full identity—until he rises in revolt against his oppressors. The Algerian psychiatrist Frantz Fanon, writing in neo-Freudian terms, even suggests that the colonial cannot become a full man until he has killed the white colonist. In similar words Freud suggested that man came to self-identity and freedom by killing the primal father.

Eldridge Cleaver, writing from the viewpoint of a Negro in America who has come to believe himself *a colonized native within the United States,* also speaks of the need for assertion that might lead to conflict on the part of the Negro. Cleaver has gone farther than most writers in analyzing the myths of present-day America, but he has also created a mythology of his own. In his 1968 essay, "The Land Question and Black Liberation,"[23] he tells us that it is hard to put into words the meaning of the murder of Martin Luther King, Jr. Cleaver declares:

> Action is all that counts now. And maybe America will understand that. I doubt it. I think that America is incapable of understanding *anything* relevant to human rights. I think that America has already committed suicide and we who now thrash within its dead body are also dead in part and parcel of the corpse. America is truly a disgusting burden upon this planet. A burden upon all humanity.[24]

Among white Americans in the 1970's there definitely seems to be a reversion in racial attitudes, a return to the racial theories of the years between 1870 and 1900. By this I mean a return to the implicit belief in the evolutionary distinctiveness of the races, especially the black and white races, with an overburden of faith in the higher intelligence and general "civilization" of the white race. The California electrical engineer with his supposed "tests" showing the lower IQ's of "pure" Negroes and the addition of one point on the IQ scale for each 1 percent of "white" blood in a "Negro" is but one clear indicator of a nationwide antiliberal trend.[25] When such beliefs led to outrages in Mississippi, we said "consider the source." What shall we say when the same beliefs lead to outrages in Pontiac, Michigan?

The sad conclusion we must reach on any objective

evaluation is that the struggle for equality not only has been thwarted by "the turn right" of the 1960's[26] but has been effectively eliminated from the mainstream of American consciousness. Racism is the rule, not the exception, in the everyday life of the United States in the troubled 1970's.

The above observation on race simply serves to illustrate the fact that when I speak of myths I do not intend to suggest that myths are false—any more than Rudolf Bultmann intended to suggest that when he spoke of "myths" in the New Testament.[27] Indeed, the fundamental way in which we experience life as human beings expresses itself in language that takes on an equally fundamental form that modern scholars have learned to call "myth." But myth is fundamentally true—that is, in the practical terms of everyday living, useful and constructive—only when it leads us on to actions and attitudes that make us more humane. The forms in which our culture expresses itself are always myths, whether we live as educated white people in the United States, as uneducated black people imprisoned in the United States, or as Algerian or West African rebels.

This is not to say that some men do not live in what the philosopher Jean-Paul Sartre would call "bad faith." Such men of cynical insight either find that the myths are broken or have given up on the faith that made those myths true and constructive. Such men may well be the kind of destructive exploiters denounced by the Marxist myth or seen among the cynical bureaucrats of the Nazi S.S. Often political leaders who wave the flag and shout pious phrases are such men of bad faith.

However, as mentioned above, there is the basic fact that a myth is no longer a myth if one recognizes the elements of unreality in it. Stephen Crites has observed that when we forget that fictitious stories are fictional, we descend to the level of myth.[28] This points out very well the fact that it is the *unconscious acceptance* of a story about one's people or the world that is the essence of living mythologically. One gets the impression that conservative defenders of the *status quo* on the one side, and people such as Cleaver on the other, are genuinely living in the world of myths. In such a situation, when the myths are negatively and inversely related to each other, as are the myths of American rectitude and black revolution, two hostile and blind parties club each other in the darkness. Their only salvation would seem to consist in coming to a consciousness of the state of unreality in which their inappropriate myths have placed them. Men forget the teaching of Tillich: *Myths can and do die.*

The problem of the twentieth century, seen from the standpoint of a student of myths and religious expression, is that we live in a time when myths of long standing are dying and myths of inadequate vitality are rapidly being born and are rapidly falling ill. The tragedy of our time is that dying and dead myths, since they do not die in every human consciousness at the same time, often seem to cause the deaths of millions of human beings.

Thus it is on the basis of essentially nineteenth-century myths that the conflicts and struggles of the twentieth century have been fought out. The conservative defenders of "the American way" are giving expression to a myth that arose in the late nineteenth century and was originally called "liberalism." The revolutionaries, both in the establishment sense of Marxism in communist countries and in the Third World sense of African and American Negro protesters, are shaping their feeling by a form of human expression best declared in the great meetings of the First and Second Internationals. Nazism and Fascism gave expression to political forms that are as old as the *Republic* of Plato and that found form in the several revolutions in Latin America in the nineteenth century. Men bring their own history into being by shaping their intentions in the mold of stories that they have made the noumenal structures of their minds. The latest thing in social development seems always a century behind the speculations of the philosophers. Perhaps Marx was wrong in saying that philosophers had only sought to understand the world before his time. I believe that philosophers do change the world just by their efforts to understand it, which provokes them mentally to create a new and ideal reality. But philosophers rarely live to see their new creations concretized in society.

It seems likely that many of the social critics who have followed my lead in pointing out that there is a new mentality or new consciousness arising in America[29] have not seen the basic significance of the religious motive in the birth of new forms of consciousness such as this. *Chicago Daily News* columnist Sydney J. Harris[30] is one who has seen this. Church history professor LeRoy Moore, Jr.,[31] is another. These two writers have seen the foundational importance of religion in cultural revolution more clearly than the best-selling authors. Moore points out that the essence of the new youth culture is a move from an older mythology of a secular or profane America to a new view of a sacred America. Moore goes on to say—accurately—that there are actually three myths instead of two in this series, which proceeds from a nineteenth-century conception (on the part of intellectuals and religious leaders only) of the American people as the new chosen people comparable to the Biblical nation Israel, to a twentieth-century vision of a secular, bureaucratic, technological society beyond the need for the crutch of religion (Reich's Consciousness II), and now to a mystical, often occult vision of America as a

Holy Place that needs to be cleansed by rites and cere-
monies as well as by the ecology and peace movements.[32]

"WE SHALL NOT BE RECONCILED"

There is a perversity in animal nature that runs
through the kingdom of life from the microscopic speck
in its mud puddle to the nuclear physicist taking his instrument readings. Living things just won't be pushed,
even for "their own good." The cat we would stroke
moves away, the child we would dress runs and hides,
the patient we would help leaves his prescription on the
shelf, untaken. Man's stubbornness is less a mark of his
transcendence than it is of his biological unity with the
rest of the blossoms on the tree of life.

Avoidance and denial are familiar patterns of behavior
to the psychologist. Men shun whatever they feel is ex-
ternally imposed or that constitutes a threat to their own
inner determination. External behavior can often be
modified by force or fear, but the inner man haughtily
remains unconvinced and silently awaits the opportunity
for rebellion. The ultimate answer to the mentality of
J. Edgar Hoover and B. F. Skinner[33] is not found in the
philosophy of the Yippie or the black revolutionary but in
the observations of Viktor Frankl, the psychiatrist and
former concentration camp inmate, in his remarkable
book *From Death-Camp to Existentialism*.[34] Man—like
his animal relatives—is more than a bundle of nerve
tissue, more than a pattern of neurons; *man—and every
living thing—is awareness of existence as choice*. Man
may be unfree, but only as the result of positive or negative decision. Life is precisely matter in the form of freedom. This being the case, it is understandable that large
social groups, made up of such irritable, self-deciding

persons, should be inherently conservative. ("Conservative" means self-sustaining, ultimately selfish.) Throughout most of human history, large groups have been welded together and brought into organized action in efficient forms only by the conditioning power of force or the threat of force (i.e., law). B. F. Skinner's injunctions to men to give up the fallacy of considering themselves free and to accept social conditioning is hardly a new gospel.[35] Such pleas have been translated into demands and these demands have been "conditioned" into action on every page of history, from the codification of law on the stela of Hammurabi to the building of the pyramids to the creation of the Nazi *Wehrmacht* to Stalin's Five-Year Plans to the killings at Kent State University, Attica prison, and a hundred places in Southeast Asia. A really new suggestion would be a psychology of spirit that makes appeal to man's higher insights, building on his inborn need for community and playing down his equally inborn aggressiveness.

In studying the social psychology of conservative groups in America a few years ago, I became quite aware of this human capacity to resist whatever is construed as "pushing," which I term *social inertia*. A social body tends to remain at rest in the absence of exterior forces that propel it out of its stasis. In the terms of a physics adapted to living organisms, this force needs to be much more than slightly greater than the weight of the inert body. The human monad (to borrow from Leibniz) has the power to push itself back (in a rough way, for one can never return to a former social condition), thus nullifying the "work" done by the propelling progressive force. Such a movement is rightly called "reactionary." But the universe of social interaction as well as the universe of physical possibility is an asymmetrical organism, its elements maldistributed throughout its area. There is never a case of equal action and reaction in the social universe, for there is an asymmetry of personal and group force existent at almost every social point. The laws of the social universe play dice (and cheat)— something Einstein declared that the God of the physical universe would never do. The laws of society are made in men's minds and are subject to the latter's constant intellectual erosion. Society's laws are also subject to being colored by the selfishness of the men and groups who attain the social power to make such laws and enforce them.

We often overlook the basic fact that the makers and guardians of the laws use every ploy they can devise to uphold their present situation. All is not only fair in war, it is also fair—or unfair—in peace. Belatedly, the public learns the truth. We are told that it was the state troopers, not the prisoners, who killed the hostages during the prison riot at Attica, New York. We are told that it was the state police who killed the students at Orangeburg, South Carolina, and at Jackson State in Mississippi. It was the National Guard that slew the young people at Kent State in Ohio. It was the Army, not the Vietcong, that slaughtered the women and children at My Lai. It is the police and the FBI, not the Mafia, who tap people's telephones, photograph them at public meetings, and "shadow" them on their daily rounds. Conservatism, resistance to changes in the *status quo*, and reaction (where it is not the result of plain ignorance and xenophobia)—these are characteristic of people holding power. No aware person needs Marx to tell him that.

Think of the most morally inferior deeds you can, and you may surprise yourself, upon investigation, when you find that such deeds are sometimes the methods of "control" and "conditioning" used by authorities in America. I am sure they must be used elsewhere as well, for America has no monopoly on perversity. This fact is no excuse, however.

A tight telephone network between the administrators of universities works to "check" on prospective teachers and is designed to keep "troublemakers" off every campus. Blacklists of "subversive" teachers, students, and visiting lecturers are circulated—but over black telephones, not on publicly passed paper. The witch-hunting in higher education in the early 1970's is not surpassed by that in government itself.

Frankly, resistance to change, which is a characteristic of all living things, becomes an utterly demonic quality on the level of humanity. On the plane of the group known as "the nation" (i.e., on the international level) such resistance and irritability expresses itself in war; on the domestic or national level it expresses itself in exploitation and repression.

How Do We Find America?

Today the United States is less a nation-state than it is the headquarters of various worldwide business cartels. Where does America begin and end? Does it not begin on the frontiers (American-guarded) of the Communist countries? Does it not even begin in the midst of the Marxist "world"? Why else does the United States plan to equip Tito's armies if the Soviet Union attacks Yugoslavia? Isn't our national boundary on the thirty-eighth parallel, where American and Korean troops guard the 1953 armistice line? Where does the United States stop and Canada begin? Even the Canadians (our biggest trading partners) see themselves as "hewers of wood (trees, lumber, wood pulp for paper) and drawers of water (electrical power)" for the American empire. Where are the clear lines of division between the United

States and the United Kingdom? Australia? New Zealand? South Vietnam?

Today the fifty United States (and the free commonwealth associated with them, Puerto Rico) stand together as the first among equals and the dominant economic force in an international alliance embracing Atlantic and Pacific. The vital issues of this symbiotic association of nations lie in the Atlantic basin and Western Europe, but increasingly the Pacific–Southeast Asian interests of the dominant member are skewing and straining the structure of this super empire. Now, with overtures toward mainland China the alliance may well be overbalancing itself. Question: In some possible future war of the Soviet Union and China, whose side would the American empire take? Remaining neutral might not be possible. In the case of the Indian-Pakistani conflict, the United States sided with that ally which is also the client of Red China.

The brokerage firm of the two super empires, the United States and the Soviet Union, is the United Nations. After many years of intransigence, the United States witnessed the admission of the third (yet only potential, not actual) superpower to the brokerage firm. The United States Government seems to have undergone a shift in consciousness about China. Just how real that change in mentality actually is will be demonstrated by the swiftness of the United States' winding down of the Vietnam War. The idea of bringing China into negotiations at the United Nations is surely good, but the question still remains, Will we and the other powers forswear war in favor of United Nations negotiations when land and fortunes are at stake?

The lesson of history may well be that men learn no lessons from history, yet one fact comes across clearly from the study of power politics. When a political-military rivalry and/or conflict has gone on for a long period, it is not ended by the disarming of one party. The idea of unilateral disarmament is idealistic—and dangerous. Whenever one party to such a rivalry has allowed itself to become weaker than the other, war has been the result. Military strength, although wasteful of needed resources, is probably a necessity now and will remain so for some decades. Only a general, worldwide scaling down of armies and missiles can change the dangerous world situation. But, as the example of Switzerland shows, it is possible to be militarily strong and peaceful at the same time. Sweden, too, is a strong, armed nation, but has lived in peace for many years. What is needed is a balanced, realistic approach to trade, economic exploitation, and interference in the affairs of others. International modesty goes a long way toward preserving peace.

America after Vietnam will have to face up to keeping a realistic balance between external relations and internal relations. America will have to be strong without being belligerent. This call for international modesty is more than a phrase. It is a strong suggestion for a way of politically being-in-the-world that is responsive to the needs and overtures of other nations without heavy involvement in external affairs. America is too large, has invested too heavily in countries all over the globe ever to be seriously isolationist again. Isolationism is as foolish a suggestion for this country as prohibition. It is wishful thinking, a schizophrenic loss of reality, not a reasonable political posture. Yet, America must now turn its primary attention to the internal war that has raged without letup since the foundation of the republic—the warfare of the powerful against the weak.

In the absence of powerful propaganda and unreasonable selfishness and fear, the events of the past decade

should convince all of us that violence and internal dis-
cord are the American way of life. Many policemen and
their fraternal groups are convinced that numbers of citizens are out to kill them when they are on duty. The
instability of the socially mobile lower and lower-middle
classes, with their penchant for scapegoating and illegal
violence, must be combated by education and social programs directed to them. The right-wing sickness signalized by Ku Klux Klan violence must be cured. The
clamor for vigorous anticommunism, with its ever-present
danger of creating a nuclear war, must be silenced. The
popular pressure that is used to support America in its
role as the policeman of the world must be relieved.
Somehow the pressure groups, pro- and anti-Israel, pro-
and anti-China *et al.*, must be democratically but firmly
curbed so that the hairs on the tail of the dog will be
stopped from wagging the very large dog. The practice
of international modesty, the maintenance of a low pro-
file, demands that. Orangeburg, South Carolina; Kent
State; Jackson State; My Lai; Soledad Prison; Attica—all
these harsh words from our internal present tell us to
turn our eyes responsibly to the wound beneath our
armor that makes our every external victory a Pyrrhic
one.

3

THE STRUGGLE FOR EQUALITY

Former Attorney General John Mitchell was once reported to have said that there is no New Left in America
but rather the United States is moving so far right it soon
won't be recognizable. America does seem to be caught
in a conservative reaction at the beginning of the 1970's.
This conservatism—like right-wing movements all over
the world—represents the philosophy of the privileged
classes but is parroted and put into action by the blue-
collar classes. These working-class whites believe that
they are privileged, even though they have little power
compared to the wealthy. In their myopic, selfish materi-
alism they often wish to deny equality to citizens who
differ from them in race, sex, religion, and political outlook. For one hundred and fifty years of American history
those who were denied equality were either silent or in-
effectual in their attempts to achieve equality. Since
the 1950's this situation has changed. The civil rights
movement, which has long since passed away after giving
birth to the Black Power and black nationalism movements, as well as inspiring the Chicano, Puerto Rican,
women's liberation, gay liberation, and Jewish Defense
League movements, is undoubtedly the major internal
event of American history since the Civil War.

The most spectacular American social spasm of the
past decade has been the growth of the middle-American

backlash. Surely, the struggle for equality has won many victories, but it has suffered a severe setback because of the political "turn right" of the 1960's.

RACISM, SEXISM, "STATUSISM"

Among groups of monkeys studied by animal psychologists there is found to be a distinct hierarchical order among males and females. The well-nourished, well-cared-for young monkey naturally falls into the ritual of showing deference before the older (and larger) males. The dominant male eats first and eats more than he needs, then he leaves the food supply for the rest of the group.[36] The human urge to create classes and ranks, status and privilege, seems to have a basis that lies at least as deep as the primate level of organic evolution. The human race is crisscrossed with divisions socially created by men on the basis of the drive to dominate or the need to acknowledge domination by others. American society has class and status divisions quite as much as Oriental and European countries have—although sometimes these lines are more subtle in America than elsewhere. Modern technological societies are made possible precisely because they create more and more subgroups by the highly developed industrial device of the division of labor. The modern university, which has become a multiversity, is a prime model of American society.[37]

Of course, the freeing of many subgroups in our culture from the need to struggle or toil constantly for the necessities of life has erased the real need for many of the divisions that exist among human beings. These continue to exist because of social inertia or culture lag. Many of the role expectations of women in America are based on this cultural inertia, and the sensing of this by some women today has produced the protests of the women's liberation movement. Advances in science and their application to industry thus erase the social need for some divisions among people and at the same time create new divisions in the social group.

The original philosophies of economics, based (as almost all were) on the concept of scarcity, also created divisions among men that may or may not have been based on genuine social needs. Such economic theories also contained (and many still contain) the notion of certain free resources such as air and water. The progress, or regress, of our industrial society has now made it clear that there are no such free resources. Unfortunately, much of industry and government still behaves as if air and water were free and unlimited and so the pollution level remains critical to world health. Pollution by noise, smoke, smog, odor, filth, and wasted landscapes has produced a new division among men—a division between those who must bear the full brunt of the blasted and poisoned environment in cities and towns and those who can afford to escape some of it.

Certainly the most devastating of all the divisions created among men in history have been those based upon race. Slavery existed from the morning of time, but it did not generally rest on racial distinctions. In comparatively modern times it came to rest almost exclusively on such distinctions. Indeed, even when the racist and the victim were actually members of the same race, as in the case of German and Pole, of Englishman and Southern Italian, of European and Turk, of Nazi German and German Jew, the false conception was invented that the exploited party was of a different race.

Such divisions as were declared to exist among men usually rested upon real social and cultural distinctions, such as skin color, language, state of technology, and social customs. None of these variables, however, with the exception of military power or the relative lack of it, suggested any inferiority on the part of the exploited group. The culturally advanced, highly artistic, well-organized tribes of West Africa, for instance, since they lacked guns, were decimated by the Portuguese, the Spanish, the English, and the Dutch, who used gun power to make millions of Africans slaves. More distinctions have been created among men by the use of force than by any other means. The similarity of this situation to that of wild monkeys should not escape notice. We also should not miss the fact that the great modern tragedy of slavery was played out in the Americas—and particularly on the soil of the United States.

THE EXPLOITATION AND EXTERMINATION OF PEOPLE

The myth of the new world as a desirable place to which to migrate has been current only for some 125 years. With the exception of true exploring types, few Europeans thought of going to the North American continent as a preferable way of life. Even in the eighteenth century, the trip across the Atlantic was dangerous. The climate in the new world was considered harsh. While there was a strong impulse in the hearts of many Catholics and some Protestants to go to America to win the heathen, the greatest impulse was that of nationalism and the desire for territory. Territory was sought not as an end in itself but as a source of riches. America was seen by the Spanish, the French, the British, and others as a great plantation that could be worked for an increase in wealth without the restrictions of custom and law that might limit such exploitation in Europe.

Since the European peoples were exploding across the entire globe at the time of the discovery of America, it was natural for them to consider moving free labor from the less desirable climate of Africa to the richer growing lands and the mineral discoveries in America. As early as 1442 the Portuguese learned to trade in African slaves. Negroes were brought to Spain, where they were bred and Christianized, and later their descendants were sent to labor in Haiti. There were so many Negroes in Haiti by 1503 that the governor requested that the trade be stopped. Even Christopher Columbus engaged in the slave trade, sending five hundred Indians to Spain in 1494. This practice was opposed by the queen. Nevertheless, Negro slavery was promoted in order to prevent the enslavement of Caribbean Indians.

The Spanish slave trade was augmented by English competition. In the early seventeenth century British America received its first slaves at Jamestown, Virginia. The date was 1619 and the transportation was by a Dutch ship. Since tobacco was the chief crop and slaves were useful in tending tobacco, slaves continued to be imported. By 1790 there were two hundred thousand Negroes in Virginia.

While there were many movements against the slave trade, and while in the late seventeenth and early eighteenth centuries various laws began to be introduced to curb slavery, it was not until after 1811 that the slave trade was ended in the British Empire. By this time the United States had been founded and slavery, with its basic challenge to the Anglo-Saxon concept of liberty, was part of the fabric of the new nation.

We have already rehearsed something of the inner history of the United States. Slavery from the beginning of American expansion into the Western lands was a bone of contention between small farmers and plantation owners, between Southerners and Northerners. Each new state as it was formed became an object of compromise between free and slave interests. Finally the continuance of slavery in the Southern states gave emotional power to an essentially economic movement that led to civil war.

The end of civil conflict did not end the problem of slavery. Slavery can be understood in two senses, the first a strictly legal one in which some human beings are legally declared to be eligible to be the property of others, the second a state of affairs in which the unrestricted exploitation of some people by others is the social custom. Lincoln ended slavery in the first sense, but not even a great war could end slavery in the second sense. Indeed the people of the North were as deeply committed to ideas of racial superiority and to a desire to exploit others as were the Southerners. On a number of occasions during and after the war, the Negroes of the North were mistreated by Union soldiers and Union citizens. Perhaps the first restrictive legislation affecting the newly granted citizenship of Negroes was passed in the North. As we have seen, both Southerners and Northerners—before, during, and after the Civil War—exploited and exterminated the Indians, who were considered so inferior that they were killed so that their lands could be stolen. This attitude and practice, which led to the near-extermination of the Indians by military force, led to the so-called Indian wars, which were not ended until 1890.

Perhaps the most shocking revelation of the new, realistic assessment of American history in the 1960's and 1970's has been the spate of books documenting the sordid, materialistic basis of the growth of the American nation. New studies in the "Negro problem" and in the history of white dealings with the Indians have made us aware that, regardless of what we were taught in school, the United States is not the land of the free and the generous but a country built on theft, slavery, mass murder, and exploitation. Whatever could be stolen from weaker people was stolen; whatever could be turned into a profit, even at the cost of men's lives, was melted down into gold. The Negroes of today and the surviving remnants of the Indian tribes are silent witnesses to a bloody, greedy history. The rock "slave" fences of Kentucky and the arrowheads picked up in plowed fields all over the country give testimony to a past that we would like to forget but that still determines the social problems of the last quarter of the twentieth century.

FACING UP TO THE PSEUDO MYTH OF EQUALITY

There is nothing wrong with the middle-American myth of human equality. It is perhaps the highest expression of the drive toward individual freedom and social opportunity that characterizes the modern history of the Northern European peoples. The concept which holds that all men are created equal and that all men have the same natural right to pursue happiness is sound and constructive. The only problem with this concept is that it originated and has continued to flourish as a partisan idea. It is a parochial idea held by the majority of Europeans (that is, whites), and it lacks a universal extension in the practical thinking of most whites that would make it a profoundly moral ideal.

While the concept of human equality is one of the most advanced and spiritual ideas of mankind, its spirituality has been limited by its partiality. Even by law, equality was denied to Negroes until the middle 1860's. Equality was denied to Indians until well into the twentieth century. And this happened in America. But the myth of America has been none other than the myth of equality. The universal equality proclaimed by the stirring words of the Revolutionary War documents was in practice restricted to whites only.

Some sociologists have suggested that socially mistreated persons who are given no indication of their residual human rights and who are kept completely under subjection rarely rebel. Rather, they observe, those exploited groups who are exposed to the rhetoric of human rights and who are given partial access to human freedom are the very ones that are likely to rebel and demand full equality. In the case of the American Negro, this insight goes a long way toward explaining American racial problems in the twentieth century. In the case of the Plains Indians in the last half of the nineteenth century, the fact that the Government signed treaties with the tribes and usually held only a portion of each tribe on the reservation, so that part of the tribe still ran free, also makes this insight sound convincing.

Perhaps the best indication of the reality and spirituality of the concept of human equality is precisely this historical evidence that *equality cannot be restricted to one group and denied to another without provoking rebellion among the exploited.* It is a living idea and worthy of being lived, not just preached and written about. The social problems of the United States in the 1970's are deeper and more complex than they are in any other country. This is so for the very reason that all parties have been widely exposed to the rhetoric of equality. This idea is abroad in the land and our social friction will not cease until equality is universal among our people and is held out as a possibility to other people.

What Is Equality for the 1970's?

Part of the problem we face in discussing equality with members of minority groups, whether these are made up of racial, national, sexual, or sexual preference groupings, is the implicit definition of the term in the minds of middle-class whites. For WASPs (and others like them), equality still has a kind of nineteenth-century liberalism attached to it. It smacks of laissez-faire, of lack of social control, of the (supposed) opportunity to rise as high in the economic and social order as one can by hard work. The problem is that the myth of equality, in this sense, was always a myth. It never has been real, except for a very few people who operated in the absence of law or despite laws.

Even more frustrating today is the acceptance of this nineteenth-century myth by middle-class blacks. On this vision is based black capitalism.

Perhaps the first thing we should say about a definition of equality that will fit the realities of America in the 1970's is that equality is not and (for the near future) can not be fact. Equality is a relative term, having to do with rank, estimation, and status. But status, or rank, with its corresponding power, is achieved in America by, with, and because of money. It takes no law to establish this, only attention to our customs. The all-pervasive power of accumulated wealth to influence American life in directions desired by it is well established.[38] We must face up to this fact: in a population of nearly 210 million, where 25.5 million subsist below the poverty line and where most people live on the bulk of their income (using up even their savings for vacations and retirement), so that the national wealth is concentrated in the hands of a few thousand people, any equality that exists is a tenuous thing. Thus America is actually divided into the poor (the lumpen proletariat, without resources), the consumers (petit bourgeois and bourgeois), and the manager-directors (capitalists and their agents). Any equality in such a situation can be brought about only by government, insofar as government can be made amenable to the will of the larger public.

Of course, this is only a description of where we are right now. Despite the novel humaneness and noble democratic idealism of our foundational documents and laws, the equality of the individual has had a checkered history in America. No time has seen more pressure on the theory of the equality of the individual than ours. For example, the pollution of our country takes place because it serves the interests of the wealthy. The rights of the many are spurned. One needs only to ask the questions: How much do your words and wishes as an individual stack up against the words and wishes of General Motors? And, If you don't want a plant put in your neighborhood, how much effect do your wishes and those of your neighbors have against the chamber of commerce, the city government, and the manufacturer? Perhaps in an upper-middle-class neighborhood the power could be generated among a large group to stop a plant from coming in. In a working class or poor neighborhood, no such influence could be generated. That all Americans are equal is not the conclusion we would draw from an objective assessment of our everyday experience.

All of us recognize the basic fact that equality is a myth in our society. We recognize this without believing that ours is a totalitarian society or wishing for violent revolution. For the aspects of life that concern the average citizen—enough food, clothing, and recreation, and decent housing—the equality quotient is unimportant. Except for the millions of poor whites, blacks, Indians, and Chicanos, most people are reasonably satisfied with their housing. America probably leads the world in the number of separate, detached dwelling houses. Yet everyone does not live in a mansion—few people do. Somehow, however, above a certain economic level, the hostility and envy of the man of lower status against the rich and powerful vanishes. It lingers as a vague dream in the minds of many and surfaces on occasion, because of luxurious associations, as envy, but in the middle-class consumer, class hatred is nonexistent. Real envy undoubtedly boils up in the very poor urban person, rarely in the rural poor. But the rural poor may rapidly be coming more like the urban poor through the radicalization that the spread of radio and television brings.

Just recognizing clearly the problem we have concerning equality in America may be all the revolution we need. A clear idea of the status of the average citizen and the relative lack of status of the poor can help us understand the problem of the lack of good legal representation and the usual failure of the poor to find justice. The whole idea of "Black Power" and the appeal of the motto "Power to the People" rest on this insight. Equality is an ideal yet to be reached in America.

EQUALITY AND THE SCHOOLS

The public schools exist (ideally) as the instrument of enlightened state power to make equality a possibility, if not a fact. When the schools are sidetracked into becoming agencies for preserving inequalities and preventing the disturbance of prevailing power relations, then those schools are the enemies of democracy. Such corruptions of the public school ideal have often been made in America. The racially segregated schools of the Southern and border states, legally (by state law) segregated along racial lines, were the classic example of this. The clearest present example is that of the de facto segregated schools of the larger Northern cities and the border states. However, schools of this sort, preserving inequality, exist all over America. The basic inequity of these institutions is not often upset by enforced integration. Rarely does busing upset the preservation of power relations either, although some *in loco* equality may be realized. The whole concept of neighborhood schools rests on the idea of preserving the *status quo* and protecting the presently existing geographic, economic, and power allocations in the community.

The Supreme Court of California recognized this fact in a 1971 decision in which it held the funding of schools by local school district property taxes to be unconstitutional. Hollywood could afford much for its schools on a low real estate tax, for instance, while the Watts area could afford little, even on a high property tax. It seems likely that this California Supreme Court ruling will influence other suits and other, similar decisions all over the country. We may be forced, legally, to turn our schools into channels for equality. The question is, Can we and will we do it?

In 1972 President Nixon suggested that perhaps the nation's entire school system (all the thousands of school districts) might have to be funded by a tax levied by and funds appropriated by the Federal Government. This might well be a useful device. I would only suggest that we should not move toward the so-called value-added tax (which originated in France) to fund the schools or to fund anything else. I say this because by its nature the value-added tax rests financially on the backs of the consumer and the poor rather than on the corporations, which have the money and power to be the equal of the Government itself. A value-added tax is merely collected by industry and commerce, not paid by them. New methods of raising funds for schools are needed, and we need to start searching now for methods that will be equitable and not new subsidies for the wealthy and powerful. Someone has said that the United States has socialism for the rich and free enterprise for the poor. That insight is not very far from the truth.

4

THE DENIAL OF PROSPERITY

Today, more than at any time since the 1930's, the average citizen can understand how the American boast of great prosperity might be challenged. The recent economic difficulties that have led to an uncertain stock market, the end of the expansion of public education, and a governmental move to control steadily rising wages through the business community have given all parties—most particularly the middle American—an increased appreciation of the fact that the United States is hardly the home of a universal prosperity. A few years ago the declaration of the civil rights movement and of church groups, backed up by sociological data, that there was "another America," which had little or no part in the loudly trumpeted "good life" in America, was greeted by derision and slanted economic charts designed to show how good life was in the United States as compared with other countries. Today, perhaps, more Americans are open to the reality of our situation and willing to see that America suffers from the same economic difficulties as other lands, although to a lesser degree.

One of the big myths accepted throughout the world is the myth of American riches. Like most myths, including the myth of equality, it contains a germ of truth. The United States is a rich country. The natural resources of its vast territories and the manifold abilities of its large

and well-educated population make it one of the wealth-
iest societies on earth. But the myth of equality does not
rest upon reality, as we have seen in the previous chapter, and neither does the myth of prosperity. The facts
are that America is potentially prosperous for all, actually
prosperous for a large segment of its population, but not
actually prosperous for all. The problems that are involved in this mythical situation that threatens to destroy
the nation are precisely these: inequality of distribution
of the actual wealth and unrealistic consumption of natural resources with too little consideration of the ill effects
on the environment.

The Locus of Suffering

The physician can often spot an infected area of the
body by its reddish discoloration and local heat. The student of American society can spot the location of social
and political problems by observing the incidence of
poverty and near-poverty among our people. Not surprisingly, the very locations and groups that figure in national problems are marked by poverty or a near approxi-
mation of it.

In this second half of the twentieth century the trouble
spots in the United States might be identified as the
slums of the great cities along with blue-collar neighbor-
hoods throughout the country; the South as a region,
particularly the Gulf South; and the Western areas,
where the remnant of the Indian population resides. If
you add to this the university and college campuses and
the upper-class suburbs of Northern cities, you will have
a map showing the location of the poor, the wealthy
conservative, and the well-off liberal classes. This is not
to say that the rest of the population is immune to the
social revolution of our time, but it is to say that here are

the major participants in the battle over economic equality that is shaping up in this decade.

Is it surprising that people in the South and in the slums of large cities everywhere are, on the whole, poor —relative to the national norm—and also largely either black or blue-collar white? Being a member of a minority group, or without the education that is the road to economic prosperity in America, is practically the same thing as being poor or at least struggling in America. We are dealing here with generalities, to be sure. The South is not all poor, and in fact along the Eastern seaboard, in Texas, and in its mountainous middle section, the South has been growing more prosperous in recent years, as compared to past decades. Industry has already become of paramount importance in the South, while the population is growing and its educational level is rising. The slums of large cities contain more than black people. There are other minority groups besides blacks and Indians, groups such as the Chicanos and the Puerto Ricans, and they have the same problems as blacks. But the concatenation of factors involving history, prejudice, and exploitation singles out the blacks and the Indians— along with the poor whites—as the symbols of the falsehood of the myth of American prosperity.

It is not surprising, either, that the same areas and the same people form the stage and the actors for the dramas of racial conflict and the sordid story of unemployment and welfare schemes. These are the 25.5 million Americans who live in relative poverty.[39] It does no good to say that the situation of the American poor person is much better than that of the poor person in Latin America or Africa. This is very probably true. But when was a comparison of the United States with an African country taken as legitimate? After all, the poor person in the United States has to live in an economy geared to prices that can be paid by those Americans who are not below the poverty line. The only adequate economic and sociological study that can be made of the poor in America is one that judges deprivation in terms relative to the American middle class.

Toward a Corporate Social Order

There are two myths of a political and economic nature that are the causes of American economic inequality and roadblocks to the solution of American economic problems. The first is the irrational hatred which the middle class and its blue-collar allies have for the theory, and even for the word, "socialism." This irrational anti-socialism is of course fostered by the public relations arms of wealthy corporations, which benefit from economic inequality. But long ago the class basis of this conservative doctrine was lost and anti-socialism became an element in the American civic religion.[40] Of course, the United States Government for decades, under the control of both political parties, has taken on the characteristics and agencies of a socialist state. But in the United States, because of the membership of the decision-making bodies, both elective and appointive, state socialism operates for the benefit of business and the wealthy and the institutions they favor, such as the university and the large transportation corporations, rather than for the benefit of the population at large. The one and only solution to the problem of economic inequality in an economy as wealthy as ours is some form of redistribution of wealth, perhaps so mild a form as the nationalization of heavy industry and transportation and a profit-sharing plan by which all citizens would profit from the functioning of these industries. Funds accruing to the Federal Government from such procedures could also finance free

medical care, welfare support, support of education, and
social security pensions. Such a program exists in the
Scandinavian countries today and does not arouse any of
the fears often voiced here of becoming a communist
society.

The second element in our economic perplexity is precisely the resistance of much of big business and of many
white-collar and blue-collar workers to the redistribution
of wealth and a guaranteed annual income. However,
America's problems are so complex and of such long
standing that nothing short of a thorough reorganization
of our form of society will overcome the inequalities now
endemic in it. Lest this be taken as Communism, we must
remember that it is the right-of-center Republican administration of President Nixon that has come out in favor of
a guaranteed annual income to replace the sordid and
dehumanizing confusion of the fifty welfare states we
presently have. Even big business should be able to see
the greater human and economic utility of such a program in place of the present inequality, which could
eventually drive the dispossessed into revolution.

The genius of socialism is its Biblical heritage, its
emphasis upon the cry for social justice which is the
historical legacy of the great prophets in the Judeo-
Christian tradition. It is this prophetic criticism to which
Marx gave modern—and secular—expression. Moreover,
the Marxian emphasis upon the individual as a cell in the
living body of a history-bearing social group is also Biblical, resting ultimately upon what Johannes Pedersen[41]
calls the Hebrew vision of corporate personality. The
vision of corporateness in the social order was deempha-
sized or lost in Western nineteenth-century thought. Indeed, it was lost throughout the West after the French
Revolution. Not surprisingly, Marx drew upon the tradition of the French Revolution in developing his "action

philosophy" in the 1860's. The real, inner strength of socialism lies not in its physical power but in the power of its truth and the efficacy of its social thought to spur society toward social justice. The Christian church must aid the West in the recovery of this social-philosophical depth, since social atomism has bled Western culture white. There is no longer much social cohesiveness or genuine group loyalty, and life has become meaningless for millions within the traditional institutions of the West. Meanwhile, demonic elements, which also entered Marxism, have deflected the social emphasis within socialist countries. There seems to be little difference between the "capitalist" and "socialist" worlds. Christianity must aid socialism in its recovery of its own genius, too.

It is not really very progressive to suggest the kind of philosophical redirection of American thought that I have given here. Actually, the knowledge that the so-called free market and competitive individualism is basically anti-Christian and antidemocratic is commonplace to the Biblical scholar, the theologian, and the social philosopher. The only democracy to be found in a social situation characterized by such elements would be power for a very few men who began the economic competition with unfair advantages over others. Observers of economic life have remarked for centuries that the rich get richer and the poor get poorer.

THE ADVANTAGE OF STATE CAPITALISM

The economy of the United States has become so complex, its public and private sectors have become so interrelated, that it is not beyond reason to call our present economic system "state capitalism." Now, state capitalism corresponds exactly to the socialist theory of central planning. Other countries quite as democratic in outlook and origin as our own have engaged in a form of state capitalism for many years. Previously we mentioned the Scandinavian countries. We should also mention the United Kingdom. That which most distinguishes a socialist form of central planning is governmental ownership of the means of heavy production, including heavy transportation.

The economic situation of the United States in the 1970's is one in which an inflationary spiral has been driving up wages and prices out of all proportion to the production of real goods and services by industry. One of the major causes of an inflationary spiral is the untoward amount of power possessed by the strong labor unions attached to the central heavy industries of the country, particularly the steel and the automotive industries. When the automotive and steel workers go out on strike demanding higher wages it is quite possible for the entire economic life of the nation to come to a standstill. This is especially true in the case of steel. However, there are other labor groups that have the power to stop the nation's economic life. These include the workers in rail and air transportation and the stevedores, who are able to paralyze water shipping. We might add to these the unions of truck drivers and other workers in overland transportation and the drivers of intercontinental passenger buses. Strikes of these workers can paralyze the life of a nation at any time.

Various Presidents and national administrations have found it necessary, for example, to take over the operation of the railroads or to intervene in dock strikes, their actions extending even to the use of military power. It is not unreasonable to assume that if the means of heavy production and transportation were nationalized, the inflationary spiral might be curbed by more severe restrictions upon strikes as well as by public notice that the profits gained from these industries are to be distributed to all citizens regardless of their place in the economic situation. This being the case, besides their regular income, workers in heavy production and transportation industries could hope for no more reward than that given to any other citizen. The justified feeling that capitalists and owners are exploiting the labor of workers in industry would be done away with. Also the tendency to set off a chain of wage increases by strikes in steel would be curbed. There would be no reason for such strikes, since they could only endanger that portion of the profits to be shared by the workers themselves.

Of course such a centralization of economic power would be subject to the possibility of abuse. To guard against such abuses should be the major consideration of the Justice Department, the Departments of Labor and Commerce, and the various security agencies of the Government. In order to prevent a monolithic governmental structure, the people should be urged to form their own consumer and worker protection groups, which could lobby in the political sense for their interests as over against those of the bureaucratic management class. No good socialist form of economy could be contemplated that would not have a built-in ombudsman system by which complaints could be lodged by any citizen against the government's management of industry and performance of other services. The kind of consumer protection agency now envisioned for the Federal Government plus the private consumer protection groups presented for our consideration by Ralph Nader and others would be useful and vital parts of such a planned, totally nationalized economic situation.

84 The Recovery of America

Selfishness and Its Victims

Traveling through America is both an enchanting and a discouraging experience. The land is beautiful where the damage that man has done to it is not too great. The vast mountain ranges with their deep valleys and snow-capped peaks inspire us. The rivers, when seen from a distance, are beautiful. Only when we come near and note their pollution do our spirits sag. But the greatest mark of the inequity of wealth in our country, the greatest mark of the foolishness of our use of our natural resources and treasure, is shown by the dilapidated conditions of our cities and our small towns. It is difficult to conceive that America is one of the richest countries on earth when we look at the state of our buildings. Our cities have their lovely downtown areas, often the result of urban renewal or other cleanup programs. But areas such as Penn Center in downtown Philadelphia or the Golden Triangle in Pittsburgh are not primarily made for human habitation. They are places to go and places to trade and, more nearly, places in which to be entertained. Our spirits cannot help being depressed as we travel through a vast conglomeration of housing and business such as that seen in the city of Chicago. The buildings are gray and black and streaked by polluted air. Surely they reflect the mood of their inhabitants.

But the dilapidation of America is not limited to the inner cities. The small towns spread across Ohio, Kentucky, Michigan, and Pennsylvania all show, in even more striking ways, neglect and a kind of exploitive overuse. These are not happy towns. There is no beauty here. Buildings are thrown up and allowed to decay and are used for all the rent and other profit that can be gotten out of them and then simply left as eyesores. How can we spend so many funds abroad, how can we invest in so many wars, how can we neglect the habitations of our spirits in this way? America's poverty is the direct result of the emphasis upon material profit alone. One wonders where this profit goes. The high rents charged the slum dweller, the high mortgage payments charged the young homeowner in the small towns and suburbs, all these monies seem not to go back into the upkeep of the land. One wonders what good money is if it is not used. America's poverty is self-made, it is a state of spirit, it is a result of greed and selfishness and blind worship of figures in bank account books. The land was and probably still is rich, but our minds and our spirits are poor.

The suggestions made in this chapter about reorganizing the political and economic systems of the United States are vague and perhaps Utopian. And yet the problems that have confounded the United States since the 1930's are such that only the most profound changes make sense as a way out of the quandary in which we find ourselves. It is clear that, as now constituted, the society, the government, and the national direction of the United States are guided by the selfish interests of those who are in positions of power due to their accumulated wealth and whose actions carry through certain forms of philosophy and economics growing out of the most selfish forms of human thought. That which is glorified as capitalism comes down to the desire to hold on to whatever one happens to possess, coupled with the privileged position necessary to insure the increase in value of such holdings.

This element of human selfishness runs deep in the American political and economic systems. Julian Bond, the young Negro representative in the Georgia legislature, has remarked that politics means the power of being able to say who gets how much of what. He further remarks that for the majority of black men it means "getting nothing from you-know-who." Such observations bear too much truth to be funny. But it is not only the black man who is effectively kept outside the mainstream of American life in the present economic order. The Chicano (or Mexican-American) until recently, when he began to organize himself, has been kept at the very bottom of economic society. To a large extent, the Chicano is still there as a hewer of wood—or better, as a picker of tomatoes and oranges. To a very large degree the Puerto Rican is effectively kept out of the mainstream of American life, despite the fact that he possesses American citizenship and did so before he came to this country. This applies even to the third generation born in this country. The Oriental, by reason of clannishness and a feeling of cultural superiority as well as by the exotic character of his race and culture, is prevented from entering into the very mainstream of the culture.

But there is a very large group of Americans, native-born and citizens all, Caucasian, and for the most part Protestant, who are still only strangers in a strange land when it comes to political and economic power. These are the white poor. The South is full of these white poor. Oftentimes they are not only the children of sharecroppers but sharecroppers themselves. They work land they do not own, receiving a miserable portion of the proceeds of the crops. The white poor also inhabit the Appalachian slums of Cincinnati, Dayton, Cleveland, Columbus, Chicago, and Detroit. It is the white poor, at the very bottom of society, from whom the members of the Ku Klux Klan are drawn in the South and Midwest, for it is such marginally effective men (in the economic sense) who most fear the economic competition of the Negro and other minority groups.

These are the white poor who have been so gullible as

to believe the propaganda of big business and the land-owners in the South and Midwest. These white poor have accepted the belief that any form of social welfare or legislation designed to redistribute the economic resources of the nation is the result of Communist plotting. These people, often displaying the most rigid and uncompromising kinds of ignorant personalities because of the fundamentalist religion that is their only cultural heritage, are their own worst enemies and thus the enemies of progress in our land.

Bob Dylan, in a famous song, sings of the white poor of the South as being "only a pawn in their game." He means by this that the white poor, stirred to racial violence by the preaching of white racist agitators, are being used to protest against the movement toward equality of the Negro, a movement that would help the poor white man as well as the poor black. These people think of themselves as the "good, sound Christians" of America. They take pride in their economic independence, which too often means only the right to live in a shack upon land that is not theirs, which they work for the benefit of the landowner. They are the good people who (although they may make moonshine whiskey) are sure that liquor is of the devil. They feel that far worse than alcohol are marijuana and other substances brought to our country by (they are sure) Communist Chinese. These are the good churchmen, adherents of a religion which has forgotten the injunction to forgive and to serve and to love but which is rigidly hostile and aggressive, breaking over easily into violence, since it is so full of the preaching of hell and the representation of God himself as vengeful and punishing. These men are the cannon fodder for America's wars; these are those who volunteer.

The poor white most often is himself a member or the

descendant of members of a Protestant sectarian group. These groups represent the ultimate divisive principle, which destroys the witnessing power of the Protestant Reformation. These sectarian groups have forgotten that *protestari,* the Latin root of the word Protestant, meant "to bear warm and positive witness." Instead, they have taken Protestant to mean denigrating and denying whatever happens to be going on in the world. The sectarian movement, which has been chronicled by historians such as Sidney Mead and theologians such as H. Richard Niebuhr, had its greatest flowering in the United States. It is a form of religious atomism, an ultimate splintering and separation of man from man. Sectarian splinter groups have produced the most atomistic or separated (one might almost say schizophrenic) spiritual personalities of any religious system in the world.

For the outer splitting of man from man and the inner splitting of man from his own finest impulses that is the result of sectarian atomism, there can be no simple political and economic solution. There must be proposed a spiritual, a theological solution, an answer drawn from the history of religion and the church, to this question which has been put to man by the demonic sectarian interpretation of Christian tradition. The only answer to the separation of man from man is the doctrine of the people of God. The church in our day must stress a churchly—that is, a corporate and social—solution to our problems, in distinction from the individualistic and atomistic solution stressed by the sect. The concept of the body of Christ, and the doctrine that those who believe in Christ are incorporated into one body in him, is the real foundation for a new and vital social and economic order. The doctrine of the body of Christ joined to a communal view of society could produce a Christian socialism that is effective against the disabling effects of selfishness in our present profit-oriented society.

RECONCILING THE CULTURE
AND THE COUNTER CULTURE

As is well known, the United States has witnessed the evolution of what commentators have come to call a counter culture in the midst of its bustling life over the last decade. The essence of this counter culture involves the allegiance on the part of many younger and older people to the ideas incorporated in what I have called "the new mentality" and what Charles Reich has called "Consciousness III." What these terms indicate is the beginning of a social movement that is not so much an opposition movement against the various political, economic, philosophical, and religious ideas of the institutions now in control of our society as it is a conscious effort to create a counter or parallel culture alongside these existing institutions.

Beyond question a counter or parallel cultural movement is under way. The institutions that are being formed theoretically and practically by this movement are actually based upon the social and communal apprehensions of Biblical theology and the socialist movement of Western Europe in the nineteenth century. The counter culture proposes to make the fact that we are dependent upon each other the central apprehension of its vision of society.

The counter culture often has been denigrated and satirized because of the vagueness and youthful idealism of its vision. To a large extent this satirization and rejection has been justified—but not because the feeling that all men are brothers, and that society should reflect this fact, is itself a ridiculous idea. The criticism has been justified because the counter culture has tended to reject reason and rationality in the undertaking of human projects. This rejection of reason, of course, would rule out any socialization and any form of government at all. However, it is easy to show that the youthful and the not-so-youthful enthusiasts for the new mentality in the counter culture have gone to the extreme. In the course of rejecting the demonic and disabling effects of technical reason upon man (as seen, for example, in the development and proliferation of weapons capable of destroying the world and in the development of a bureaucracy that dehumanizes and takes the joy out of living throughout the civilized world), the counter culture has failed to see that technical reason is not all there is to reason among men. To use the terms of theologian Paul Tillich, the counter culture has rejected technical reason, autonomous reason, but it has forgotten ontological reason or theonomous reason. This is to say, the counter culture has identified all reason with the absurdities and the devilries of the bureaucratic culture of modern society in both East and West.

But it is precisely man's rationality that makes it possible for him to see the gap between what he and his society really are and what they could, under the impression of a more total view of reason, become. The theologian and the philosopher who have identified with the desire of the people of the counter culture to find a more human mode of living must help these people to see that man has a reason that goes beyond the bare bones of technical reason or human logic. Theologians and philosophers of the future should continue to point up the shortcomings of the bureaucratic state that has been built. The theologian particularly should try to show how devilish the modern conception of charity and welfare has become. The theologian should point out what love among brothers, and in a family setting—even when that family is two hundred million strong—could be.

But the theologian and the philosopher dare not think these tasks complete when they have criticized the failures of autonomous or individual reason and the peculiar failures of bureaucratic or technical reason. Rather, we must expect that the intellectuals of the counter culture will point to the depths of the human experience which brings into play the richness of ontological reason. This is the reason out of which, we are told by the Scriptures, God himself comes into the world—the Logos, or Word, or reason of God. This is why we are told that man, under the impression of the divine Spirit, can become ecstatic and filled with heavenly love and blessing. Man captured by the idea of God and his Kingdom can achieve a theonomous or God-governed reason. It is this reason which Anselm speaks of when he begins his arguments for God's existence, saying that he believes in order to understand. That is, as he goes on to say, he is a man of faith seeking understanding for his faith. What the modern world needs is a theologian and philosopher who will show us that he believes that God is love and that God has created mankind as brothers and sisters and who then goes on to try to find out how this can be made clear and practical in the everyday world. Only such a depth of philosophical and theological insight will help the counter culture to become more than a parallel set of institutions that will exist simply as colonies within the body of the established mother country.

Very shortly the United States will celebrate its 200th anniversary. Two hundred years is a short time in the history of a great people and in the history of a nation. Several European nations go back for over a thousand years. Chinese history spans several thousand years. And yet the United States is not a young country. Most of the countries that are now members of the United Nations are countries that have existed only since World War II. The United States Government is one of the oldest governments in the world having a continuous existence in its present form. Two hundred years have seen a number of experiments tried in this country. Perhaps the crisis of the 1960's and 1970's, the crisis of the last portion of the twentieth century, has shown that the experiments have not all been successful. Now that we are nearing our 200th anniversary it is time to turn to the completion of the task that the American people set for themselves when they decided they would establish a country that would have liberty and justice and equality for all.

5

THE ABUSE OF LAW AND ORDER

The cry for "law and order" in the early and middle 1960's was really a call for the reestablishment of de facto segregation in schools and the preservation of whites-only suburbs.[42] The movement of President Nixon in 1972 to "do something" about court-ordered busing is clear evidence of this. Court-ordered busing is law, but it is not the "order" most whites want. It was strange that no hue and cry went up at the time about white crime, and especially none about white-collar crime. The Federal Government, through the Omnibus Crime Control Bill, has been beefing up local police forces with automatic weapons, gas guns, and radio equipment. Large city police forces now have riot formations and counterinsurgency gear that makes them small armies in themselves. Somehow, these formations and this gear seem to be used chiefly in black, Chicano, and university youth communities. The very idea that there is white organized crime is said to be false by federal officials.

It is strange and difficult for me to come to the conclusions about the representatives of the law in the United States that the events of the past decade have forced me to. I was reared, through my formative teens, in a policeman's home. That man, though no blood relation to me, cared for me and sent me to high school. He was a good, honest cop. Maybe now it makes sense that he never was promoted. I more or less grew up with policemen. The police station, rides in a police car, free passes to the circus, the fair, and ball games—all the things a policeman's kid used to get in a quiet city—were well known to me. I never knew what it was to fear cops, much less to hate them.

Perhaps my views began to change a little when I was in the Marine Corps. Marines often stand guard duty and serve as military police. I worked with local police, for short periods, in both Japan and the United States. Actually, the police we worked with in Japan were but soldiers under a cover name, for Japan at that time was occupied and supposedly had no army. The police in the United States revealed themselves as less friendly, more inclined to be brutal, or at least very much more rough, than I had suspected as a policeman's kid. Once I was the sergeant of the guard over a naval brig. I remember a poor, skinny, middle-aged man who was brought in scared and shaking after he had been picked up by federal agents and the civilian police as a deserter from World War II. It was 1952 and he had been "over the hill" since 1944. He was somehow pathetic and seemed relieved to be with soldiers again and away from the police. Actually, all of us felt sorry for the man. He said we treated him better than the police had done.

In the mid-1960's the student demonstrations began. The civil rights movement had started earlier, but it had affected, in the Deep South where I was living at the time, only black campuses. In the days of the original student strikes over the Vietnam War, because of foolish university policies and growing sympathy with the black struggle, white faculty members and students began to learn what the blacks had always known: that the police enjoy throwing their weight around. They feel that human rights are what the police allow, not what the Constitution and common sense guarantee.

The 1950's and 1960's saw the use of water hoses, clubs, tear gas, and fierce police dogs on civil rights demonstrators; the use of pepper gas, nausea gas, CS, and other combat-type tear gasses on college and peace demonstrators; the killing of black students at Orangeburg, South Carolina, and Jackson, Mississippi, by state police; the beating of innocent bystanders, peace demonstrators, and even delegates to the 1968 Democratic convention in Chicago; and finally the fatal shooting of four white students at Kent State by the Ohio National Guard. These and hundreds of other frightening events have simply wiped out the credibility of the lawfulness and fairness of the police and other security forces of the country in the minds of many. The FBI, forced into a grotesque posture of narrow-minded, sexless, "young businessmen" conformity by its director, the late J. Edgar Hoover, has lost the mystique of respect it had when I was a boy. The fact that the FBI agents in the South are said to have sided with the police and segregationist politicians and offered little protection to blacks and white civil rights workers, not even working very hard to solve the murders of several black and white liberals, further demolished the public's respect for the FBI. Then the revelations that the FBI, Army intelligence, and other security agencies had been actively spying upon college professors, college students, civil rights activists, peace demonstrators, and even members of Congress who opposed some governmental war policies further depleted whatever residual confidence large sectors of the American public had in the existence of true freedom and justice in America.

Somehow the governments, state and federal, the Establishment at all levels, seemed determined to introduce beliefs and practices that had no place in normal American life but were more typical of European tyrannies. Even the legendary Royal Canadian Mounted Police, across the border, out of the direct line of command from Washington, was made to lose its luster. Canadian parliamentarians themselves raised a cry that the RCMP were illegally capturing American "draft dodgers" and turning them over to the FBI at the border in contravention of Canadian law. Like spoiled children, determined to break every piece of china in the dining room, the men in power in America themselves smeared merd across the face of every law enforcement agent, then blamed the young, the pacifists, the civil rights activists, and the intellectuals for this destruction of integrity and respect. It will be a long time before the officers of the law are able to recover the respect that proper enforcement of sensible laws would naturally receive.

Rough and Quick Justice for Some

We must go back into the history of the United States in order to get a clearer view of the outcry of many middle-class and lower-middle-class whites for law and order during the 1960's. We should assess the Western movies that are such a large part of our culture and that affect the appraisal of American culture by Europeans. These movies are taken by many to show that the United States is now and always has been a violent country. The cowboy settled his grievances with a gun. Justice was rough and quick, administered without any particular attention to the subtle nuances of right and wrong. The only way one could be sure that law (supposedly) was being served and the lawless were being punished in the Western movie (at least until the rise of the "psychological Western") was by the convention that the good guys always wore white hats. We might observe cynically that in the America of the 1960's and 1970's, in public opinion, the bad guys always seem to be black.

Attorney General John Mitchell convinced Congress to pass legislation allowing "no-knock" entry of people's dwellings in the District of Columbia. So-called preventive detention laws for the District of Columbia were also passed. The "no-knock" procedure was extended throughout the United States as a part of the Comprehensive Drug Abuse Prevention and Control Act of 1970. Under its provisions federal narcotics agents may enter people's homes without search warrants when they suspect the presence of drugs. Senator Sam Ervin of North Carolina, himself no liberal but a strict constructionist, fought against these legislative efforts tooth and claw. "No-knock" effectively means the kind of tactic made legendary by the Gestapo, the tactic by which the Secret Police enter one's home without warning in the middle of the night. It is claimed that the use of marijuana and drugs is such a threat to our society, and it is so easy for those who use and abuse them to flush them down the toilet when they hear the police coming, that the police simply must have this "no-knock" law. It seems to me that the greater danger to the United States would be in having such Gestapo-like laws. "Preventive detention" is a way of saying that the Constitutional safeguards against being held without bail or being held under excessively high bail would be overridden. A person would be held without the possibility of bail if the police thought that he was capable of committing a crime while he was out on bail or that he would attempt to escape the reaches of the court. Again, it is interesting to note that the District of Columbia is something over 70 percent black and that preventive detention and the "no-knock" laws are directed particularly against blacks.

THE POLICY OF DESTROYING TO SAVE

We should not overlook the serious threat to the integrity of the law as well as to respect for the law on the part of progressive persons and youth that is posed by the "marijuana laws." The heartache caused by unreasonable laws against what is, at worst, self-abuse cannot be calculated. The sight of police drug raids against students while the Mafia drug traffic operates at top capacity and white-collar crime increases is ridiculous. If the marijuana laws were repealed and marijuana (while not necessarily being legalized) were combated by social educational programs strongly assisted by the churches, the power for good of the police would be magnified many times.

Certainly the widespread use of marijuana and drugs (for marijuana is not a drug) has brought a good deal of suffering into the United States. I do not want to defend the use of marijuana and certainly not the abuse of drugs. But on the other hand, some of the aggressively totalitarian tactics designed by the police to combat drugs are potentially more socially dangerous than drugs themselves.

This is a point that can be easily covered up by the emotionalism of the various federal agencies and the moralistic response of ministers and mothers. It is not necessary to defend the use of even a nondrug such as marijuana in order to criticize the kinds of laws that have been passed to combat addictive and destructive drugs, which are a real problem. All one needs is a logical approach to life. Such a logical approach would tell us that it is not necessary to destroy the laws and the social system of the United States in order to combat a social problem. The kind of logic that would defend unlawful laws in order to combat a menace such as hard drugs is akin to the logic of the artillery officer who reported, with a straight face, that it was necessary to destroy a certain Vietnamese village in order to save it. We may very well destroy the fabric of United States society try-ing to save it from drugs. The only possible answer to the drug problem is education and treatment. These forms of care for persons preclude the use of punishment and fear, which are the major ingredients of the "no-knock" laws. The example of Prohibition should teach the United States once and for all that one cannot stop a widespread social problem with the use of fear, scare tactics, and tough laws.

No man in possession of his faculties will do violence to his own nature or interest. From this basic psychologi-cal foundation, all laws should be erected. When men feel that they must go against their own future welfare by violating certain laws, it is clear that those laws are abnormal, unnatural, and destructive of their personali-ties. Why have so many of our citizens found it to be either in accordance with their natures, or an agreeable violation of their natures, to break the laws in recent decades? To try to answer that question means going in search of the whole American experience over the past several decades, for no particular life history (i.e., indi-vidual history) could give a valid answer. Let us ex-amine America's recent social atmosphere in hopes of some clues.

The chief question in the consciousness-searching game that most intellectual Americans are playing with themselves these days seems to be, What went wrong, and when and where and how and why? Perhaps the only direct answers to that question will be given in

BIBLIOTHECA

Ottaviensis

parlors and family rooms while people are playing intellectual games, or as part of the small talk at cocktail parties. There simply do not exist straightforward, direct, or even checkable kinds of answers to questions as massive as this one.

THE PARALYSIS OF MORAL COMPUNCTION

What went wrong could be seen going wrong in the earliest American diplomatic, economic, and military mistakes made after World War II. These mistakes forced the Allies—the nations that had cooperated to defeat Nazi Germany—into an open rupture in 1947. This gave birth to the Cold War. Those political, economic, and military kinds of mistakes probably hinged on a mistaken apprehension of the motivations of Joseph Stalin and of the Communist regime in the Soviet Union in World War II. Our acquiescence in the division of Europe in an arbitrary fashion right through the middle of an industrialized nation of over 60 million citizens was unparalleled in stupidity. This set the stage for abrasive relations between the Soviet Union and the Western democracies that could only predetermine a negative future. These kinds of political and military mistakes were pointed out ahead of time by a number of commentators, and in this regard some conservative Army generals were more right than wrong when they protested against the withdrawing of American and other Allied forces from central Europe back to arbitrary lines of demarcation.

In any event, the unsettled situation in central Europe, particularly in Germany after 1945, set the stage for a large number of what can only be called schoolboy shoving incidents between the American—and also the British and French—military forces and their Russian counterparts. These kinds of gratuitous insults and other difficulties laid upon one another out of jealousy or ignorance of each other's motives (or out of some base political motivation) set the stage for what has been called the Berlin Blockade of 1947. After the blockading of Berlin, there set in instantly a paralysis of normal American life. Only those old enough to have lived through this period can recognize that this was true. It was not a slow, creeping kind of illness and hatred but an almost instantaneous paralysis of American moral compunction as it related to the Russians. It was as if a rattlesnake had injected a huge quantity of venom into the body politic. This is no defense of the Russians or what they did. To criticize the Soviet Union would take another book. The "when," then, was 1947.

There is an old legend which holds that you either die right away from a rattlesnake bite or you suffer a lot and get over it so that you are able to navigate. The situation of the United States after the Cold War started was analogous to that of a human being who had been bitten by a venomous snake. The venom turned the health of the nation around. I can remember that a sort of sinking feeling came over everyone, as if to say, "Oh no, we just cleared away all that mess two years ago and here it has started all over again." And yet our dander was up and we had the invincible belief that we had won World War II all by ourselves and nobody was going to push us around. At the time we may have been more than half right. If we hadn't won the war all by ourselves (the Russians were very much interested in letting the rest of the world know that we hadn't), at any rate we had come out the big winners in terms of surviving with relatively little damage. I don't believe it was World War II that poisoned American society. If that had been the case, Canada wouldn't have escaped, for Canada was in that war more than two years longer than the United States. It was the Cold War that poisoned American society. It was not the conflict so much as the moral erosion—the undermining of our belief in anything but ourselves and our need to defend ourselves against some rival creed—that sapped our moral energy and strength.

How Evil Sometimes Leads to Good

The moral theologian is so used to the ambiguities and the relativities of human morality and even of the application of divine commandments to the human situation that what passes as strange contradiction to others is routine paradox to him. The moral theologian knows that sometimes good leads to evil and evil leads to good. In the Cold War, as in World War II a few years before, evil led to a rather large amount of social good. The good that came out of evil was the same in both cases. The American upper and middle classes, the owners of business and the directors of the military, had to mobilize the entire society to be the bastion of defense for democracy again. Since we were to be the arsenal of democracy, we needed the black citizen as well as the white. From the late 1940's through the early 1950's, culminating in 1954 in the Supreme Court ruling that racial segregation in the public schools is unconstitutional, we saw the gain of a great number of civil rights by black United States citizens. However, as I have observed elsewhere, and as black writers themselves have observed in *The Black Revolution*,[43] the victories of the civil rights movement were also defeats.

The Supreme Court decision of 1954 and other decisions handed down in various courts concerning the rights and privileges of Negro citizens ultimately were disastrous because they provoked a cold, calculated, aggressive hostility in both North and South that was determined to resist the tide of Supreme Court decisions. The vilification of the justices of the Supreme Court is well known. Not only the radical right but the conservative middle had much to say about the qualifications of the justices who handed down decisions concerning segregation. Far beyond this, there were apparent in both North and South calculated attempts of a significant majority of the American people to resist the clear legal and moral extension of the warrants of the United States Constitution and Bill of Rights, founded though they were on Anglo-Saxon common law, to the case of Negro citizens. Do we any longer need to stress that this resistance to the full extension of the constitutional guarantees is as strong above the Ohio River as it is below it? These constitutional decisions were legal, paper, or surface victories. The fact that society itself didn't change and that opportunities for blacks did not change generated within the black community its own brand of demonic, aggressive hostility. This I would name the third toxic poison that has marred the health of the American body politic. The first was the coming of the Cold War; the second, the hostile resistance to the Supreme Court decision concerning integration; and the third, the natural reaction of large groups of blacks in the ghettos to white resistance to their full citizenship. These three elements make a very potent brew. We have been half drunk on it in America for a decade and a half.

But there are light elements as well as heavy ones in the drama of recent history that has resulted in our present social situation. The lighter elements, perhaps, are the forces of education and awareness that arose with the large number of young people who flocked into the institutions of higher education, the state-supported universities and community colleges. With the extension to millions of young people of the kinds of sensitivity and awareness that genuine college work can give the human mind, an increasing social consciousness developed in America. This social sensitivity, fostered by the better influences of higher education, had earlier made the young blacks in Greensboro, North Carolina, so aware and socially sensitive that they began the sit-in movement. It was among just such kinds of people that the support came for the 1956 Birmingham bus boycott led by Martin Luther King, Jr. And this social awareness, while not entirely color blind, was not prejudiced. It was found among Gentiles and Jews, Northerners and Southerners, whites and blacks. This social awareness spread itself beyond the color question, particularly in the early 1960's when it looked as if most legal battles had been won in principle, and the liberals began to rest upon their oars. Then the awareness began to spread to the overseas involvement of the United States in the Cold War.

The year 1961, we must remember, was the beginning of the sending, under President John F. Kennedy, of relatively large numbers of military advisers to South Vietnam. This awareness of social issues also overlapped into the environmental field. The good influence of social sensitivity and heightened sensibilities, the gifts of a university education, must be seen as lighter but nevertheless increasingly more significant elements in the complex situation that has brought American society to its present state. By 1964 both the toxic elements and the benign elements, all the confusions and the sensitivities, the awarenesses and the ignorances were joined together and America resembled a vast social time bomb.

Good had come out of evil. At least legally and for the liberal middle, the racial issue was solved. Unfortunately it was not solved for those who profited economically, socially, and egotistically from racial discrimination. It was not solved for those who directed great amounts of business in this country, nor for blue-collar workers, who increasingly felt their position on the job jeopardized by Negro competition. Above all, the racial issue wasn't solved for the black. And so evil came out of good, too.

The evil that came out of good must be seen as an ironic thing. The evil of which I speak is social conflict. Tinder had been laid for the fire, and the matches were upon the mantelpiece. For a long while no one seemed to know where the matches were, but now they knew. The young people who began the bus boycotts and the sit-ins, the first blockage of troop trains in California and the first moratoriums, now knew where the matches were. The flames of conflict were lit.

I am not implying that this is a drama without its heavies and heroes, or that from the standpoint of the historian or the sociologist there are no villains. Those who have become increasingly self-aware and socially aware are not to be castigated for what they have done. Nevertheless the motives of all of us are mixed, and the results of our actions can only be guessed at—they cannot be known. Looking back now, over this brief span of time, we can see that the match was laid to the fire and that the fire has yet to be put out.

Toward a More Humane Public Morality

Speaking of public morals, one of the most difficult things to understand and comprehend about our society is that there seems to be no middle ground between the hokey, phony innocence of the Walt Disney cartoon or movie and the outright pornography of the "triple X"-rated movie. Even those movies and other kinds of entertainment that do fill that gap tend to be heavily oriented in one direction or another. Now the world is not full of people who believe that squirrels talk or that mice sail boats; so Walt Disney films leave much to be desired. But I don't think it is full of people who are that skin-conscious, either. One wonders, then, if there is any significance to be found in examining some of the kinds of events that have led to the present dominance of the "triple X" and "four X" movie in our urban centers.

Several years ago the Danes decided that police forces had more to do than monitor films, books, magazines, and posters, so they legalized pornography. They also had the Northern European finesse and skill to conduct some sociological research upon the topic first, later basing their new laws on it. One of the more interesting and hopeful signs that have arisen out of that sociological research, some of which was performed by the police departments themselves, is that the legalization of pornography can be, in some measure, brought into a statistical harmony with a decrease in sex-related crimes. This is a heartening sign of social health.

I certainly do not hold with censorship in any respect. Nevertheless, for the sake of children, if for no other reason, there should be a brake on the presentation by the mass media of violence and the physical side of sexuality. This brake will be effective, however, only when it is self-imposed by booksellers and film producers, because of their reading of the taste, the real desires of the public.

The people must begin now to exert pressure in political ways upon state legislatures and upon Congress to move American law out of the enshrined "Mrs. Grundyism," the sheer Victorianism, that dominates it. Our public laws are far more bluenosed than any of our present private and public customs. It is amazing to consider the activities that are considered crimes. Private acts between married couples, acts that are increasing in interest for many people, are crimes that—if discovered—are punishable by long jail terms. Many actions are not covered specifically by any law but are often called "illegal" under catchall laws such as "disturbing the peace" or "vagrancy."

Citizens must rise and demand a new, more humane morality. As it is now, the people are repressed both by those who break serious laws and by those who enforce Victorian laws. Among the changes that should be demanded are prison reforms, removal of all legal prohibitions of premarital and extramarital sex, and the reduction or abolition of all penalties presently enforced for the simple possession and use of marijuana. In domestic law, every state should move immediately to the California-pioneered "no-fault" divorce procedure. Under this plan, "irreconcilable differences," sworn to by one spouse, are grounds enough to claim, and get, a divorce. These "differences" need not be specified, so charges of and proof of adultery, cruelty, etc., are no longer needed. This is a fine example of a modern, humane law.

"Crime" in America, with rare exception, is something committed by the poor and members of minorities. More often than not, the actual depredations committed by minority people are against each other. Most murders, rapes, and assaults by blacks, for example, are against other blacks.[44]

Young people reared in circumstances of poverty are much more likely to come to the attention of the police than are middle- or upper-class youngsters. Poor youth play in the streets, live in crowded conditions, are subject to harassment and molestation by adults and to the scorn of the police. Incidents that pass without official notice among the middle class (such as pranks, loud parties, youthful drunkenness) are often the occasion for arrests of the poor. Particularly in the overcrowded inner city there is no room for the natural high spirits of youth or the everyday quarrels of the family without infringement on others' rights or living space. Petty thievery is an ever-present temptation for those who are deprived of so much, especially when all the luxury goods of the country are displayed daily on television. It is not hard to see that much of the statistical evidence for high crime rates in cities is a record of prejudiced and inhuman response to the exploited and dispossessed of American society. There are sociological reasons, correctable causes, for the so-called high crime rate in the United States.

I have deliberately approached the various problems in America in the broadest possible way and have even given the context of world affairs for the breakdown of law and order. There is a reason for all this, and it is the simple one that life is all of a piece. Not long ago one of the television networks presented a program entitled *Suffer the Little Children,* which was concerned with the communal violence in Northern Ireland. This program showed how the children of Northern Ireland—children exactly like children in our own streets—play with toy guns and mimic adult attitudes of hatred, then are tragically subjected to bombings and sniper fire because of the senselessness of the adult world they inhabit. The children couldn't say why they hated the other party in the dispute and seemed embarrassed by the question. To them, as children, and to unthinking older people everywhere, "that's just the way things are." The lesson is plain. When the social atmosphere is full of fear and animosity, and adults engage in warlike talk or activities or both, then all social cohesion and civilized respect for law and order disappears. The only order that can be enforced is the order of superior force. And this in the last analysis is only brutality unless it is fully understood why force is needed at any juncture. Children are not capable of understanding these reasons. To them the police or soldiers are the good guys only when they are said to be. When children are told that the police are bad, as Catholic children in Northern Ireland are told, then they are bad. A policeman is a hero or a pig according to the social context. Of course, the police can make themselves pigs by their prejudicial actions against minority youth or teen-agers caught with drugs. People respond to the social cues around them, whether by absorbing adult attitudes or by responding to the treatment given them by those in authority.

Violence Only Begets Violence

It should be clear that the so-called rising crime rate in America is something for which there are a variety of sociological reasons and that the chief basis of it has been the atmosphere of violence that has been cultivated in the United States since World War II. The cult of violence has grown to tremendous proportions in this country, and those who speak of harsher legislation and shooting to kill, etc., rather than doing anything positive to lower the crime rate, are actually feeding it. Whatever makes the use of force seem respectable and escalates force as an element in human life makes might seem right and makes civilization, more and more, an impossible task.

Looked at in this way, the preaching of peace and the depreciation of violence, both legal and illegal, domestic and foreign, is the major general treatment for the breakdown of law. This is the case because a breakdown of law is actually a breakdown of civilization. Civilization ultimately consists in the practice on a general scale, and in an everyday fashion, of the virtues taught by Christianity and the other great religions. Civilization does not consist in doing what you are told, for that is characteristic of an animal-training ring, a prison, or an army camp. Civilization consists, in essence, of the multitudinous activities that follow in human life from the assent of the individual to the proposition that man cannot live alone. At base, civilization is the practical application of the golden rule of all the higher religions. Beyond all the laws stands the injunction to treat one's neighbor as one would himself be treated. Rousseau called this the social contract; Moses called it the covenant of Israel; Jefferson and Franklin called it the Declaration of Independence. As sentimental as it sounds, it is nevertheless true. Without this assent, which is very often an unconscious one, simply learned and silently accepted by the child in the family, there is no law but only the rule of the stronger in social chaos. One cannot glorify the chaos of every man against every other, or of the rigid order imposed by the police state, by calling it "the law of nature" or "the law of the jungle." Actually, nature knows no such chaos among the other species, and the jungle is well regulated by the unwritten principles of the survival of all species. The only proper term for the condition of mankind when it has violated the covenants of civilization and the human piety of comradeship that lies at the base of all societies is *sin*.

Until we return again in our attitudes and our public and private speech to the piety of comradeship and to a reasonable explanation as to why certain conduct is desirable and other behavior is undesirable, we will not live under the rule of law. Appropriations for larger police forces, the development and dissemination of more and more efficient weapons of police control and surveillance will not restore to us the rule of law. A spirit that implies, "You will do what I say or I will catch you and punish you," will only make crime more widespread. The police and the military spy upon the conduct of large numbers of citizens in an effort to enforce laws against attitudes and forms of behavior that have no victims beyond the persons involved in the behavior. The very idea of this being done will create not criminals but a criminal society. A criminal society is one in which all social relations are based on naked authority, without the consent of the governed. Unfortunately, in a number of areas today, such as efforts to control minority populations in ghettos and efforts to control youthful drug abuse, we are close to such a criminal society. In such a situation, both the police and the lawbreaker are agents of social destruction, so that the human race cannot win no matter who is victorious. If the lawbreaker escapes detection or is able to bring superior force to bear on the police at particular times, or if the police are able to capture the lawbreaker, it makes no difference. The rule of law is not established. Making the police more powerful and efficient, as is often suggested by some leaders today, cannot break the vicious circle of social destruction. The country simply slips deeper and deeper into a kind of civil war with totalitarians on one side and anarchists on the other. The only way to live under law is to escape this vicious circle by a more humane conception of what order is and by an educational effort stemming from the home, the church, the school, and the agencies of government.

In considering the problem of "law and order" in 1970, I had the following to say in *The Turn Right:*

Let there be no mistake, law and order are not necessarily the same ideals. We need to be very philosophical here, for in the popular speech of American English, 'law' is often used to refer to the regularity of order men find in the physical world. We therefore speak in American English of the law of gravity when we mean the regularity of the pull of the earth upon any material object in its vicinity. But the laws of man that create society are not necessarily regularities of an invariable kind. Not even the laws against universally disapproved actions such as murder are unexceptionable, else they could never be broken. No, law, while it undoubtedly brings the security of order out of social chaos in many respects, is still not the same thing as order. Laws are made to free men from fear— from fear of one another and from fear of those things which can be guarded against, such as the building of open fires in an urban area. Laws may even create disorder, in the sense that laws are historically made to free man. For example, the laws that did away with slavery freed the Negroes from the regimentation and order imposed on them by their masters. It certainly created disorder to free these men and women, allowing them to drift down the roads freely without a possession to their name. But what the slaves wanted was *law and justice,* not law and order. The opposite of law is not disorder, it is lawlessness. The opposite of order is not lawlessness, it is disorder. The opposite of lawlessness is not order, but law. What we want are open structures in this country built upon acknowledged covenants that hold up justice as the great ideal, not order and conformity.[45]

I still believe that this analysis is right.

6

THE MISUNDERSTANDING
OF EDUCATION

No industry in America (with the possible exception of the military industry) is quite so vast as the education industry, which former Representative Bella Abzug of New York declares has assets of 250 billion dollars and owns real estate equal in area to the State of New York. A cursory glance around the country would lead one to believe that education outdoes, in money, land, and power over human beings, even the military establishment with whom it does so much business.

Consider these facts. Education is the largest single recipient of tax funds from local governmental units, and it takes a lion's share of state budgets. Not even the military draft has the unquestioned right to require the allegiance and daily attendance of *all* young people, five days a week, nine months or more a year, from age six to age sixteen. Education is often said to be for life, but actually, for millions of Americans, education *is* life. It is the only life most Americans know until they are at least eighteen years of age. The person who has made his way from first grade through high school, gone into the Armed Forces (where he likely was sent to various schools or training programs), and returned to enter college under a government program, may find himself at the age of twenty-five or later with absolutely no experience of the world beyond education, unless he was unfortunate enough to have suffered combat.

Education is to American society what the "bush school" of the witch doctors is to African tribal society. It is more ritual and magic than efficacy. The vital question of efficacy—that is, how successful our nationwide attempts to "educate" the young really are—is the question most often asked by government officials and individual taxpayers. Sociologist Christopher Jencks, for example, has argued in his book *Inequality: A Reassessment of the Effect of Family and Schooling in America* that schools do almost nothing to close the gap between rich and poor. (*Time* magazine, September 18, 1972, p. 41.) "Tax revolts" against local school bond levies and even school operating budgets have taken place from Toledo, Ohio, to St. Louis, Missouri, and points east, west, north, and south.

My own four children had their 1971–1972 school year made traumatic by a confused school schedule in northwest Ohio. The voters refused to approve the 1972 school budget in not one, but three referendums. Finally, the teachers and maintenance personnel went out on strike, too, which added to the children's distress. America's "school crisis" is not the product of a public relations man's—or a writer's—imagination.

As a simple example of the overwhelming portion of the national wealth that is devoted to education, consider that the average increase in expenditure by state governments for state colleges and universities in the biennium 1971–1972 over the biennium 1969–1970 was 24 percent. This is only for public colleges and universities and excludes all private and church-related colleges and universities, the service academies supported directly by the Federal Government, and all secondary and elementary education.

For the 1971–1972 biennium, Ohio, for example, made a 23 percent increase, authorizing a total expenditure of 294 million dollars for state colleges and universities. For the same biennium, Indiana increased its appropriations for public higher education by 30 percent, West Virginia and Kentucky each by 26 percent, Michigan by 24 percent, Pennsylvania by 10 percent, Massachusetts by 52 percent, California by 14 percent, and Alaska by 64 percent.[46] When we consider these percentages and figures, the commitment of our society to education becomes vividly clear.

America's Love Affair with Education

It comes as a surprise to some to learn that the United States is not, statistically, the most literate nation in the world. Actually, France surpasses the United States. The exact figures for literacy (in 1970): the United States, 97.6 percent; France, 100 percent. There are actually nine countries with 100 percent literacy, France being the largest of them.[47] Japan's literacy is exceedingly high, but recent figures are not available.

Despite resistant pockets of illiteracy in the Appalachian region, on Indian reservations, and in the slums, the United States, with a population of nearly 210 million, has done a good job of reaching 97.6 percent literacy. It has paid out a king's ransom every year, however, to achieve this level of knowledge. State funds for public elementary and secondary education in the United States in 1969–1970 ranged from New York's $1,237 per pupil to Alabama's $438 per pupil, with the United States average being $783 per pupil. National figures for public schools in the United States during the same period included the following: There were 18,224 operating public school districts, 1,835,626 classrooms in use, 29,151,-

131 elementary pupils, 18,086,956 secondary pupils, and 2,219,015 principals, supervisors, and teachers working at an average salary of around $8,500 per year. There were 2,640,338 public high school graduates. Figures for the private schools in the United States included 4,200,000 elementary pupils, 1,400,000 secondary pupils, 146,000 elementary teachers, and 80,000 secondary teachers—in order to get complete figures on the educational establishment in America.[48]

Combining the figures gives us the extraordinary figure of 52,838,087 pupils in public and private elementary and secondary schools in the United States. Education is a big business in America!

Colleges and universities in the United States number 2,525, of which 1,060 are public. These institutions enrolled 7,916,991 students in the fall of 1969. They graduated 764,185 students with the bachelor's degree; 193,-756 with the master's degree and 26,188 with the doctor's degree in 1968–1969.[49]

American universities had a very tumultuous decade, 1960–1970. Perhaps for the first time the state university and the church-supported college became topics of interest for all parts of the community. The universities, like Topsy, had just grown, from the years during World War II until the 1960's, with a rate of support that increased significantly every year. The article of faith in the American creed that rather naïvely held that "education equals social salvation" prevented any real check on the rapid expansion of campuses. During the period of campus unrest, however, it became clear that (according to the lower-middle-class interpretation of events) the young people on campus have become so divorced from life that they do not appreciate what the taxpayers are doing for them. Only the shock of finding this out made the electorate at large take any interest in the campus.

Before the period of campus unrest only sports fans and alumni had paid attention, and their interest had been limited to the record of the football and basketball teams. The decade of campus violence came to an end after the 1970–1971 school year, although campus unrest did not.

The long series of disturbances on campus precipitated by the Vietnam War had quieted until the spring of 1970. There were some protests against the war from time to time, but the stepping down from the presidency of Lyndon Johnson and the election of Richard Nixon on the basis of his promise to end the war had cooled the campus scene. Then President Nixon ordered the invasion of Cambodia and a sudden wave of demonstrations engulfed hundreds of universities. Rather than understanding the disappointment of the students and allowing for that, the President set the tone for a harsh put-down of these demonstrations. The National Guard was brought to a number of campuses, and at Kent State University in Ohio, on May 4, 1970, the National Guard's mishandling of the situation resulted in the fatal shooting of four students and the wounding of several others. A few days later, two black students at Jackson State College in Mississippi were killed by state police, and the university system throughout the country was more or less brought to a standstill.

The fact that the Ohio killings were politically connected and the Mississippi killings were racially connected brings out the full dimensions of the problem of American higher education. The burning of a building housing the Bank of America at Santa Barbara, California, in February, 1970, and the bombing of a U.S. Army mathematics center at the University of Wisconsin in August, 1970 (the latter involving the death of a research fellow), were carried out as protests against the heavy involvement of higher education with big business, the military, and other aspects of the Federal Government. Some of these elements seem inclined toward racial and generational intolerance.

The public university was relatively quiet during the 1971–1972 academic year, although problems have not disappeared and the much-publicized efforts of the university to study its own nature have produced nothing but verbiage until now. Even a small institution such as the well-known Berea College in Berea, Kentucky, supposedly devoted to educating the Appalachian poor and, in recent years, to educating blacks, experienced rather serious problems in late 1971. Black students, irritated by the campus administration and incensed by the small, very Southern community in which the college is located, brought out firearms and forced the administration to suspend school without final examinations. The campus opened only after the Christmas and New Year's holidays. It is likely that racial problems will continue to plague higher education even when the Asian war is finally concluded. High schools such as those in Lima, Ohio, and several towns in Michigan have also experienced racial strife.

The American college and university are very overpriced toys. Unfaithful to their mission to be places of quiet thought, these institutions have gone in search of more and more money, more and more students, more and more buildings, without much concern for what good they could do the people they were supposed to serve.

Higher education in America is perhaps the biggest hoax yet sold to the American people, as Jerald Brauer, professor of church history at the University of Chicago told an audience celebrating the inauguration of a new president at Findlay College, Findlay, Ohio. Brauer pointed out that tax dollars are being spent to build larger and more state universities that are choking off the American system of private higher education. States are ignoring the excellence already achieved by many private institutions, opting for a monolithic system of state educational systems, where everyone copies everyone else. In Brauer's view, "America desperately needs a reaffirmation of genuine pluralism;" American education and American democracy depend on the continuance of viable alternatives.

The poet William Cohen once looked at the many impressive buildings near completion on a campus of a large regional university near troubled Berea College and observed, "When the body of brick and glass has been all erected, and every building named after the cheap politicians, the students and faculty, looking at the sterile monuments, will say, 'No,' and the spirit departs."

That is largely true. Our unprecedented expenditures to support higher education have built hundreds of buildings that are nothing but buildings, for education has nothing to do with the efficiency of the plant or the freshness of the paint. Education is an invisible commodity.

WHY UNIVERSAL LEARNING?

The professional educator, when pressed to defend the practice of educating, will make many learned and pious references to Socrates and Pluto and the aim of education in ancient Greece. That is, if he has learned enough philosophy to know anything about Plato. Actually, the superstitious American belief in the efficacy of education has nothing to do with the European tradition of Greek and Latin learning and little to do with the Christian (especially Catholic) educational tradition, which aimed to initiate all men into the mystery of faith. One root of the superstitious American devotion to education was the sectarian, Protestant background of so many of our Northern European settlers. These Calvinists, Lutherans, and free churchmen in general had come out of a religious tradition that was less interested in the initiation of the young into the mystery of faith than in seeing that everyone could read so that he could study the Scriptures for himself. The first American schools (aside from those designed to educate the future clergy and lawyers) were established to teach boys to read and write. This ideal of universal literacy—or perhaps we should say, of literacy for free white males—was a good one, of course. It became a secularized ideal when it was recognized that only the man able to read and write would be able to take a responsible part in the political life of the nation. This was, however, only one of the twin roots of the American myth of learning.

The other root of the American educational superstition we owe to the homeland of its much-publicized belief in democratic equality and political liberty, eighteenth-century France. This is the romantic vision of man as a noble savage in his natural state—the message of Rousseau's *Émile.* Rousseau stressed the wholly good nature of the child, who must be encouraged to develop naturally into a law-abiding man. This vision is certainly the second root of the American myth of learning. Certainly, we must see that the teacher having the greatest philosophical and practical influence on American public education, John Dewey (1859–1952), was indebted to Rousseau. So, too, was another famous teacher whose doctrines have been widely influential upon American private education, Maria Montessori (1870–1952).

I am not going to claim that there are not other factors at work in the American myth of education, but these two—the Protestant sectarian desire to see all men able to read, and the French romantic notion that the child is wholly good and needs only to be guided toward a constructive maturity—are the twin pillars of the activity on which our nation expends most of its anxiety and interest and the better part of its gross national product. Perhaps William James, himself a professor and a product of both American and European education, was too close to the forest to see the trees—i.e., too close to see that education is the moral equivalent of war in terms of interest, planning, personnel, and money, not to mention that it is war's equal in its potential for dizzying victory and the most brutal and stupid defeats. I have sometimes thought that America's greatest mistake was that the sheer magnitude of natural resources and talents on this continent had caused it to try to be preeminent both in war and in education. Perhaps no society can afford both. Perhaps no society needs either of these social activities. At least, no society needs them in the extreme degree to which they have been practiced by the United States.

To the twin mythological roots of America's dedication to universal education—the Protestant sectarian and the French romantic philosophies—the twentieth century, after Sputnik (the symbol of the Soviet Union's scientific "forced march" to outdistance the United States as the world's paramount nation), contributed the theosophical belief that "knowledge is power." Education became more highly subsidized by government than ever before, particularly in the areas of science and mathematics. The United States, deliberately and with loudly voiced announcements of its intentions, totally mobilized American education to provide it with the trained manpower to win the Cold War and to protect "private enterprise" from the state socialism of Communism. In so doing, the

American leadership class prostituted the very idea, as well as the practice, of education in this country and set the stage for the Dr. Strangelove tryouts of new munitions, weapons, concepts, and techniques in the Vietnam War. Also in so doing, America's leadership class created the so-called "generation gap," the oversized university, the professor moonlighting on government contracts. It guaranteed the emotional hysteria needed to make the Cold War very hot indeed in Korea, the Dominican Republic, Lebanon, the Congo, Cuba, and throughout Indochina. It was this total gearing up to outdo the Russians and not just the penny-ante ROTC program, which was mostly on third-class campuses anyway, that radicalized thousands of college students in the 1960's.

The university, preeminently, was supposed to be dedicated to the arts of civilization. The arts of civilization are not arts of war; quite to the contrary, these arts—which include all the sciences—are arts of peace. When the Romans finally broke through all the scientific "secret weapons" that Archimedes had made for his master, the tyrant of Syracuse, they found Archimedes sitting by his sandbox contemplating the circles he had drawn there. "Don't disturb my circles" were his last words as the soldiers killed him. Archimedes was only the first of a long line of scientists, stretching down to the fathers of the atomic bomb, who were to learn, always too late, the fact that the use of man's art and science in war destroys a man, destroys art, and destroys science—equally.

The university, and the American people, must remember that the arts of civilization are the embodiment of those activities which all men seek and enjoy. They are the expression of full physical, mental, and spiritual development: the enjoyment of sexuality, the engagements of friendship, obligation, marriage (in whatever form), and perhaps, for some, the sign of the fullest commitment to the uncertain future—the rearing of sons and daughters. Against such arts there can not be any natural law, there must not be any human law.

To practice the arts of civilization (which may or may not be best done through a formal educational system) —this is the form of genuine religion, the meaning of the human adventure, and much more than the moral equivalent of war. What America needs now—while its formal educational system is so captivated by dedication to war and social control—are countersystems of living and learning dedicated to the practice of the arts of civilization, for they are the arts of life.

The Shape of a Civilizing Education

At the risk of sounding trendish, I would observe that education is too important to leave to that shadow class of the academic world, the professional educators. I say "shadow class," for that is the most honorable term one can objectively place upon the holders of the so-called education degrees which, along with various "programs," have proliferated at regional cow colleges turned "universities" and are designed to staff the monstrous organs of public education in America. Degrees offered include bachelor of arts and bachelor of science in education, bachelor of science in physical education, master of arts in teaching (M.A.T.), master of education (M.Ed.), doctor of education (Ed.D.), and even doctor of philosophy in higher education. If one adds further fanciful degree titles in educational administration, educational psychology, special education, etc., one sees the wisdom of the serious recommendation that universities offer only one or two "degrees." These "education" degrees generally are but pale imitations of the traditional degrees once awarded by American universities, which patterned their bachelor's and master's programs on the British (Oxford and Cambridge) system and their Ph.D. programs on the German doctoral system.

The shadow quality, the shallowness, of these degrees becomes apparent when one examines the requirements for their attainment. Usually no languages or, at best, only one, are required, even for the doctor's degree. Little or no study of mathematics is required unless one is going to teach that subject, or, amazingly, unless one is going to be a primary school teacher. The mathematics courses for these prospective teachers are, however, generally "watered down" and not of usual university stature. This also holds true for courses in the life sciences and in physics and chemistry. Physics becomes "physical science," biology becomes "animal science," and botany becomes "plant science." History, sociology, political science, economics, and philosophy are bled white, melted down into a few sets of truisms and made into "social studies." Music, art, literature, and drama are run through the mindless, reductionistic meatgrinder of "academic" committee meetings and become "humanities." The student, generally, becomes very bored with such courses and, failing to be challenged by the real meat of their subjects, goes out into life—and probably into teaching—with only this "introduction" to the arts of civilization and the treasures of the human heritage.

Enough, for all I can say here is that the legislatures of the fifty states ought to rise up in responsible rage at the mindless waste of tax funds on the proliferation of such courses, programs, and "degrees." Enough, for the taxpayers of each local school district ought to demand by tax revolt and by pressure on their representatives that public school teachers be better educated than they are. Enough—for millions, hundreds of millions of dollars could be saved, and wisely so, if the states were made to close all but the major arts and sciences universities (i.e., those which are allowed to offer Ph.D.'s in subject-matter fields), were made to eliminate all special "educational" departments and courses except those devoted to training in pedagogical methods, and were encouraged to develop the two-year community colleges (now spreading widely as a third level of higher education) as "feeders" for the central university. The present wasteful and inefficient strategy of three overlapping systems—the university system, the state college system (now generally called "universities" or "regional universities"), and the community or junior college system—simply must be pared down to one well-planned, humanly and financially efficient program of public enlightenment. There is no state so large in area or population today—given our rapid mobility by auto and airplane—that could not be served by one single university "consortium" (or associated feeder college) system. The various professional schools for medicine, law, veterinary medicine, dentistry, and even the ministry (where suitable church-state separation agreements could be worked out) could be associated with the central university. The contents of the program leading to either a bachelor's or a master's degree in any subject could be standardized throughout the state system, and eventually throughout the country. This would agree with the program for degrees in most advanced countries.

Enormous savings would be realized by dropping those courses and programs which could be safely and easily eliminated, reducing the number of faculty members needed, and eliminating useless and costly duplication of programs from campus to campus in the same geographical area. If the useless "gut" courses such as "health" and the many "physical education" courses now offered were also to be dropped, the savings to the state and to the student would be even greater.

It would not be difficult to cut the length of time needed to earn an A.B. degree from four to three years without a loss and perhaps with a gain in the quality of the education received. In Canada, where the British model is followed more closely, one earns an A.B. degree in three years and then goes on to study a fourth year if one desires an A.B. "with honors." Unfortunately, our third-rate state or "regional" universities are now offering master's degrees in education for one additional year of study beyond the bachelor's degree. Such degrees qualify the recipient for only one thing, a higher salary in public school teaching.

The reform of American education will be advanced but not completed by the elimination of the vast "shadow structure" of the professional educational establishment. The hard decision must be made that the public universities shall practice the arts of civilization and no longer serve as institutions geared to fight the Cold War on the one hand and to "baby-sit" with the youthful surplus labor force on the other. The university must push away the box of government chocolates that it is "hooked" on and sever its ties to the very real military-industrial complex. President Dwight D. Eisenhower, once also president of Columbia University, was not seeing things that aren't there when he warned the nation against the growth and power of this force in American life. It might even be called the "educational-military-industrial complex," because the hardware, techniques, and personnel for both the warlords and the captains of industry come from the educational establishment. Dozens of reporters have documented the heavy involvement of even the most "liberal" universities in the development of weapons and the training of manpower for the Pentagon. The ROTC building on campus is but the tip of the military-industrial iceberg sticking up above the "educational" waters. We will not have a university at all if we do not separate the place of research, discovery, creativity, and learning from the place of war-related activities. It may be perfectly just for the Government to carry on some of these activities, but they should be done on army posts, in government centers, off the campus. Let him who is hungry to eat the king's bread and earn the king's shilling go about it honorably, wearing the king's uniform and not disguised in the robes of the peaceful don.

All that has been said here about research and training for the Department of Defense is meant to apply equally to the Department of Justice. It may be a good thing to educate policemen, but the university is not the proper setting for it. Unfortunately for the country, the so-called programs of and courses in "law enforcement" seem to be as trivial and fund-wasting as the programs in education. The content and expectation of courses in "police psychology," "introduction to law enforcement," and dozens of others better suited to a series of lectures at the police academy, amount to an insult to the intelligent professional policeman or university professor. Perhaps the best we can hope for is a generation of policemen and public school teachers who will be able to talk to each other, if only at the level of popular psychology and simplified mathematics.

The real diet that the university must be forced to follow will come only after it has been made to give up the overfattening government program of contract, grant, and subsidy. The university system will have to have some of its millions of students wrung out of its bloated body. These students, by the way, will be delighted to be set free, once our society publicly acknowledges that one does not have to have a university degree to be socially and economically "saved." The opening of genuine alternative routes to full social acceptance and to the finest economic opportunities will free hundreds of thousands of unwilling scholars and bored young men and women from the drudgery of "faking it" through some forty "college level" courses to earn a degree.

Do you think this is an exaggeration? Then consider the opening of term-paper-writing businesses in university towns in the East and the Midwest. Consider the underground but real business of ghostwriting doctoral dissertations. This is not an empty declaration. Fourteen years of college, university, and seminary teaching have brought a number of these cases to my attention. I must say that all the doctoral dissertations I have ever heard of being ghostwritten were in education, as only a specialist in one of the subject areas (such as English or physics) could write a dissertation in that area. People who buy term papers and pay anywhere from five hundred to ten thousand dollars to have doctoral dissertations written, join fraternities and sororities in order to have access to "frat files" on examinations, steal copies of final examinations, carry "skinnies" or cheating sheets or answer cards into examinations, try to bribe or otherwise please their teachers in order to pass courses, etc., are not happy in the university and do not really want to attend it. In my time—and every teacher could add to this—I have heard of "students" stealing the safe from a university biology office in order to see the final examinations, seen boys with special heels on their shoes, out of which a roll of white cloth with written answers could be pulled, and heard of dozens of other ways to crib on tests. Compared to these activities, the result of young people being forced to attend the university against their will, I think that the so-called violence of campus unrest is a peccadillo. We can build a university building again, if it is unfortunately destroyed, but we cannot build a university that had had its heart, its reason for being, bled white by its transformation into a moving conveyor belt into the higher-paying positions of a corrupt society dominated by business and the military. We have passed the day when all a school needed was a good teacher on one end of a log and a good student on the other, but we still need good students, interested students, and good, creative teachers much more than corps of students, companies of teachers, and a proliferation of modern buildings. As an environmental reclamation, so in education: we could make a hell of a lot of progress by doing a lot of subtraction.

EDUCATION IS LIFE;
IT IS NOT PREPARATION FOR LIFE

John Dewey was gloriously right when he was right, just as he was monstrously wrong when he was wrong. Like all creative men, leaders and molders of their times, he did nothing by half measures. When he had the truth he created, when he had hold of a half-truth, he destroyed creativity on a magnificent scale. Dewey's essential premise was that education is preparation for life and that therefore the student should practice the arts of democracy. This was a great insight, but a half-truth. Students should practice the arts of democracy, but more, they should practice all the arts of civilization. Beyond this, Dewey (and his followers) were wrong in thinking that education is preparation for life. It is nothing of the kind. *Education is life, and in a civilized community, life is education.* I cannot recall a single day of the fourteen years I spent as a student in institutions of higher education (three universities, two seminaries) that was a preparation for anything beyond itself at the time. I cannot recall a single day that continued to be useful throughout the rest of life. Perhaps it is only "watered down," homogenized courses that "prepare" one for life, because their artificiality patently marks them as nonliving while they are "taken." Education, in the root sense, means to be led out, to be taken by the hand by the pedagogue, the guide, and walked with through the streets of life. In many ways the rebelling students, the nonstudent hangers-on, the angry graduate students and assistant professors who "closed down" university after university in the 1960's, knew more of the reality of the university than the deans and provosts did. They knew that the life of a military researcher on the campus, the life of an ROTC instructor, the life of an inculcator of conformity (this applied to many of the faculty)—each was a fake life and, as an unexamined life, not worth living.

I think that Socrates, if he were to return to life and view our universities and colleges today, would laugh out loud, if he could refrain from weeping. I know many excellent teachers who do weep over our corrupt educational Jerusalem, and I weep with them.

7

THE MYSTIQUE OF THE FUTURE

The basic motivation of Western civilization seems to be preparation for the future. Governments, armies, corporations, universities, unions, families, and individuals spend a large part of every day preparing for tomorrow. The foundation of capitalism is the saving or retention of part of this world's goods for "investment," i.e., for reservation for future use, or for "seed money" to ensure the continuation of the present standard of living and production in an uncertain future. Trying to limn the vague outlines of the future that lies before us is perhaps the single largest industry in Western culture. The workmen in this industry include presidents and prime ministers, cabinet members, bureaucrats, political scientists, generals, business executives, advertising men, engineers, professors, sociologists, historians, psychologists, medical doctors, philosophers, economists, management specialists, statisticians, ministers, theologians, newspaper editors and columnists and, above all, writers, from journalists to novelists.

Underlying this superlative mountain of activity is the belief that there will be an indefinite future and that it will be more or less like the present and the past. Basic to the predictive sciences is the unexamined belief in the practicality and wholesomeness of the corporate manipulation of men, animals, and elements toward structural unities considered desirable by the group doing the planning. Also part of the core of this mystique is the belief that the future is characterized by an increasing rapidity of technological change and the growth of ever more subtle manipulative techniques. The future is not the future for most Western men with "future shock."[50] That a future without decisive change is possible never occurs to the Western mind—at least not until the enormity of the ecological crisis dawns upon an intellectual here and there. Yet the prophets of the population explosion and the ecological crisis tell us that the future for Western man may indeed be marked by the subtraction, not the multiplication, of worldly goods and by a deceleration of technological development rather than an endless acceleration.

The future need not be a "growth future," in and of itself, as the study of "primitive" people such as the Stone Age tribes of New Guinea and the Philippines and the Aymara Indians of Peru demonstrates.[51] Surviving Stone Age peoples, as well as the Eskimos (where they have not been debased by modern technology and mores) and the Aymara Indians, have adjusted themselves to a wholly different kind of future from that typically envisioned in our culture. For them the future is but a matter of the continual survival of the tribe. The future will be like the present and the past, and this is considered good. These folk have found an immanent transcendence that has no place for anxiety about and planning for the future.[52]

The point to be made is that the usual Western view of the future is a peculiar, self-elected concept, only one of a number of alternative visions of the meaning and possibility of the future.

A writer in *Pastoral Counseling*[53] entitled his article "The Theological Views of Some of My Mentally Re-

tarded Friends." Of course it was a serious essay and
useful for the counselor. I don't mean to disparage it in
the least, yet I can't help seeing the title as a fit judgment
on some of the prophets of the future, both ecclesiastical
and secular, who dominate our times. Writers on "the
theology of hope" and "future shock" seem out of touch
with reality in some of their judgments.

Myths—or better, symbolic concepts of the future—
generally fall into three main categories. Theologians
have considered these visions of the future under the
heading of the discipline of eschatology, but secular
philosophers are still so new at the generalized predic-
tion game that they have no science as yet, using only
such terms as "futuristics." Let us understand now that
the secular prophet of the future has bought in on the
theological game of eschatology, whether he recognizes
it or not.

The three categories of eschatological expectation are:
(1) the future as *devolution,* or the doctrine of impend-
ing human ruin; (2) the future as the *continuation* of the
present historical conflict; and (3) the future as *progressive evolution,* or the doctrine of salvation within human
history (realized eschatology). The religious and philosophical history of the West has been chiefly characterized by concepts one and three.

"You have been weighed in the balances and found
wanting." "Repent, for the kingdom of heaven is at
hand." These warnings, together with references to "the
wrath to come," are expressions of the Biblical prophetic
faith that the future was one of devolution. To a large
degree, the devolutionary vision of the human future has
provided the motivational power for sectarian reactions
and for reform movements within the church and within
secular society throughout the Christian era. The negative future view also gave the striking power of convic-

tion to the messages of the Old Testament prophets. In a basic sense, John the Baptist and Jesus the Christ stood in the devolutionary tradition of the minor and major Hebrew prophets who preceded them. "O Jerusalem, Jerusalem," Jesus lamented over the capital of his people. Luther, in the same devolutionary line, once observed that, for the Christian, the world is an inn and the devil is the innkeeper. The imagery of the preaching of the Jehovah's Witnesses, of the Seventh-Day Adventists, and of other adventist and pentecostal groups follows directly from the rhetoric of the Old and New Testaments and of the Protestant Reformers.

It is the duty of the systematic theologian to help men sort out their theological ideas, testing them for consistency, coherence, relevance, and faithfulness to the main insights of religion. In a way, the theologian does for ultimate concerns (i.e., theological doctrines) and ideas derived therefrom what the psychiatrist does for the confused feelings and ideas of disturbed persons. In the case of doctrines of the future, it is simple to sort out the political positions that rest upon devolutionary premises from those which rest upon progressive premises.

The vision of the future that holds to a coherent, consistent, almost static continuation of present historical conflicts into an indefinite future is basically a conservative philosophy of history. The belief that "what has been is now and ever shall be" is more Hindu and Buddhist than Western Christian.

INTROSPECTION AND ANNIVERSARIES

America will be two hundred years old as a nation in 1976. A nation born in confusion and contention, from within whose boundaries thousands of citizens (the Tories) migrated to Canada after having fought to prevent its separation from the British Empire, America will celebrate its 200th anniversary in a similar confusion. Ironically, the plastic, fabricated "history" of the nation that had been taught to so many generations of unsuspecting school children has been exposed as false in the years since 1954 (the year the Supreme Court decided that the Constitution applied to everyone). Now, in the 1970's, the clear and cold light of the truth—that this is a confused and chaotic country with more than equality for some (the white and the wealthy) and less than equality for most (the black poor, the white poor, Chicanos, rural people, and students)—shines over the industry-blighted landscape.

The cry of "Power to the People" has not ceased. Whereas it was once called out by urban blacks in the riots of the 1960's, it is now a quiet affirmation by millions of blacks, white youth, and Chicanos in the 1970's. John W. Gardner, chairman of the lobbying group known as Common Cause, located the source of the sense of estrangement that fills many citizens today when he observed for *Look* magazine: "The access of people to power is blocked by the access of money to power."[54]

Bella S. Abzug, congresswoman from New York, in the same group of interviews for *Look*, gave her feelings about the group that wields power in America:

> The thing that struck me most when I came to Congress—although I knew that we were only 13 women in Congress, representing 51 percent of the population, and only 13 Blacks (a symbolic baker's dozen of each) and very few other minorities—was that essentially we had very few young people in Congress, and no people who represented the working person. It's a middle-aged, middle-class, white male power structure; no wonder it's been so totally unresponsive to the needs of this country for so long.[55]

The Rev. Jesse Jackson, director of Operation PUSH (People United to Save Humanity) in Chicago, declared that the nation needs a "new political third force," which would represent this majority of the population that is not now truly represented in Washington. Jackson suggested that the third force might try to "run" a black candidate for president in 1972, a woman for president in 1976, and a black or an American Indian for attorney general. The mark of how far we really are from a democracy is seen when one reflects on how far-out these ideas seem to most of us. Other countries have multi-racial politics—our own state of Hawaii has it—but the thought of "running" a black even for the vice-presidency made the liberal Senator Edwin Muskie confess that America wasn't ready for that.

George Wald, professor of biology at Harvard University, declared in the same symposium: "Our task now, in a sense, is to repossess America, to try to regain the American tradition, which has been badly eroded in recent years."[56] Wald is so acute in his analysis of the future business of America that I would like to quote him further. He believes that the American tradition has been damaged or lost, and he gives his reasons:

> We have a generation of young people who, because they've never known anything else, think that certain practices that have come into our country only since World War II have always been there—that they're part of the American tradition, whereas in fact they do it enormous violence.
>
> The very thought that we could have become a country with, by now, 23 years of compulsory military service, a kind of permanent draft—nothing could be more un-American. There were generations of immigrants who came from Central Europe and Russia to escape compul-

sory military service. Now we have it, in peacetime and wartime alike.

There's been a very serious erosion of our judicial procedures. Justice in our courts has become, for one thing, frightfully expensive. And just very recently, many new practices have come in that harass and imprison people without due process—such matters as detention while awaiting trial in overcrowded calendars, excessive bail, the government's bringing people to trial on preposterous and ill-prepared charges—charges that are eventually dismissed, but in the course of the trial, a contempt citation will succeed in jailing them anyway.

We once represented a kind of beacon light to the world, and all the world looked to us for things that Americans were proud of and I hope will be proud of again—our sense of human liberty, justice, generosity. I think we no longer quite represent these things as we did, but rather great wealth, great power, great greed. And so, if we're to be proud of our country again, I think a great many fundamental changes need to be made—so fundamental as to constitute a continuance of the American Revolution. No revolution is permanent and we need to renew ours.[57]

FUTURE SHOCK AND MODERN TIMES

One of the most influential books of recent years is Alvin Toffler's *Future Shock*.[58] This book appeared in serial form in *Playboy* magazine, has been purchased by national fraternities for use in their instructional programs, and is a topic of concern for the editors of denominational religious literature. Toffler has created an interesting book that has the virtue of accumulating a mass of disconnected fact into a readable whole. Basically, he forces us to face up to the fact that the future is here, and that its problems are our problems in the present.

What does Toffler mean by this? He means that a decisive change has taken place in history, a change that makes obsolete all prior wisdom about life, government, science, and technology. Toffler is, in a word, announcing the present existence of what I baptized "the new mentality" in 1969.

Looking at human experience through the conceptual lens that Toffler furnishes us, we can see that this is indeed a new world and that our only hope lies in the spread of the new consciousness among all people. Toffler, in reference to a striking statement by Kenneth Boulding, comments, "In effect, our century represents The Great Median Strip running down the center of human history."[59] Boulding, speaking of his birth earlier in the century, says: "The world of today . . . is as different from the world in which I was born as that world was from Julius Caesar's. I was born in the middle of human history, to date, roughly. Almost as much has happened since I was born as happened before."[60]

Others have had the same impression about life in the past five decades as Toffler and Boulding. It is the case that, as recently as the time of the American Civil War, men still fought battles with sharp-edged weapons, riding on horseback, and that thousands of men died of simple wounds and from uncomplicated diseases. At home, the highest technology was only then bringing in gaslight, and millions lived in log cabins or sod houses miles from the nearest settlement. Of course, the steam engine and the telegraph were in existence, but apart from that the world of 1861–1865 looked very much like the world of the fifth century B.C.

In less than a century, the steam engine gave way to electricity and the internal combustion engine. In the briefest possible time, the jet engine appeared and then the nuclear reactor. The world's history has indeed been

divided into two parts by the acceleration of technological change, and Toffler now stands as a prophet announcing the third part into which history is divided—
the era of superindustrialism. The mark of this change is
shown by the productivity of Western agriculture, for
within a few decades, agriculture, which was the foundation on which civilization was built, has lost its preeminence as the activity of most men in country after country. Recent reports of the superabundant harvest of
grains in India (which has always been known for fa-
mine) show us that this agricultural revolution—
whereby a manifold harvest is produced by a small labor
force—is not limited to the West. The people of the
world need to take note of the "green" revolution of
scientific agriculture.

WHAT KIND OF SOCIETY SHOULD WE HAVE IN THE FUTURE?

The society of the future should be a pluralistic one.
Men of open minds and good will recognize that we
must have a society that is open—that is, full of many
alternative pathways to economic security and social acceptance. "Open" has become a common word during a
decade in which much of the older openness of American society is disappearing. The underbrush of varied
possibilities into which the rabbits of youth could run
and hide in the past has been bulldozed down by the
machinery of governmental and scholastic bureaucracy,
which has literally reshaped the earth into uninhabitable
patterns. The psychosocial motivation behind the movement back to the land among college faculty and students (the "greening" syndrome) is an attempt to "open
up," to free, to create alternative pathways to maturity
and security, to plant some weeds and underbrush into

which men and women can flee from the deadly conformity of American life.

Restrictions kill. Conformity stupefies. Regularity puts to sleep. The uninspired character of modern life has been often remarked upon. The lack of feeling, the absence of emotional tone in the bureaucratic day-to-day routine of the urban white-collar worker is well known. The discipline of the industrial or factory worker, praised by Karl Marx—and satirized by Charlie Chaplin in the movie *Modern Times*—is as nothing compared to the drowning of humanity required of the executive or professional. The student in high school and college, when he sees this embalming of live spirit and flesh, quite healthily wants to rebel against the plastic, soft-lined prison of our civilization. For millions, America has become a prison without walls.

This critique of our present *1984*-like culture is, of course, based primarily on the situation in America, and its application is limited to highly developed countries. What possibilities of openness there are in less industrialized countries I cannot say, but I think the restrictions are there too, although of a different order. We must recall that much of our critique is based on the thinking of a youth movement limited to the highly developed countries of North America and Europe. We need to bear in mind that the revolution in sexual behavior through which we are passing is more one of frankness and openness than it is one of actually changed behavior. The ideas we form about the most desirable future for man must not leave out any insights just because they are culture-centered. But we must also embrace more universal ideas. Such universal ideas must take account of the potentialities for a fuller life, such as the green revolution of increased grain production, the ultimate control of the population explosion by medical means, and the expansion of American superindustrialism (in Toffler's phrase)—or the total automation of industrial production. It must deal, too, with the irreconcilable elements in world affairs, elements such as the Arab-Israeli hostilities, the worldwide competition between the United States and the Soviet Union, the nationalistic explosion in Asia and Africa, and the problems of the control of nuclear weapons. Anyone can write of an idealized, fantastic future. Our task as religiously and socially mature men and women is to outline the lineaments of a realistic, viable future. We want to hold out the idea of a future that lies within man's reach, even if it is now beyond man's grasp.

A SOCIETY OF REDRESSED GRIEVANCES

It is not realistic to maintain that we should ignore the loud, protesting voices that assault us from every side. If it is nothing else, ours is a day in which neither individualism nor nationalism is supreme but, rather, *tribalism is paramount*. By tribalism I mean the claims to uniqueness and independent status of smaller groups of human beings than those that usually make up nation-states. It seems that it is the attraction of tribalism in this sense that has brought on the claims for independence on the part of smaller and smaller groups in Africa, Asia, and elsewhere in the world and the claims for increased political power within established nations such as the United States and Canada. We are familiar with the phenomenon of the ministate, of which many have been established since World War II. We are equally familiar with the demands of minorities within established democratic countries for increased recognition of their status as distinct political groups. The German-speaking minority in northern Italy, the French-speaking citizens of Canada, and the black and American Indian citizens of the United States are clear examples of this latter phenomenon.

In the latter half of the twentieth century all the age-old divisions of men seem to take on a sharper focus around the edges, seem to divide man from man in nation after nation, colony after colony, all around the world. Why this should be so I cannot say. Perhaps the spirit cannot come to its fullness in man unless all his unique characteristics are fully developed, including his tribal social characteristics. Whatever the reason may be, the Indian subcontinent saw the separation of its people into Moslem and Hindu groups. This split the very struggle for independence that had been headed by Mahatma Gandhi and led to a bloody war at the partition and granting of independence to Hindu India and Moslem Pakistan. In a very real way, the Hindu and Moslem struggle against the British colonial government was the model for all the revolutions and colonial struggles for independence after 1945, many of which were relatively peaceful. Their model was the peaceful revolution in India, with its occasional blood baths. The automatic granting of independence by the United States to the Philippine Islands in 1945 was not the model. This independence for the Philippine Islands was due long before the coming of war in 1941 and was given at the end of a bloody conflict in which the Philippines suffered heavily. It did little to exonerate the United States from the guilt of imperialism that taking over those many islands in 1898–1899 had earned it.

The many colonial struggles that went on in Algeria, in Indochina, in Nigeria (with Biafra seceding from the Nigerian federation later), and the host of troubles that continue in Mozambique, Portuguese Guinea, Angola, and elsewhere, are well known. The internal struggles within established states, with little or no intention of fomenting civil war or of dividing the territory, also are known to us. But these events may not be correlated with the similar kinds of tribal or group movements that produced the independence of the many former colonies. We must, however, see these two things as a unity. The struggle for black equality in America goes back many decades. Like so many vital movements, it has roots in Biblical Christianity and the influence of Biblical religion upon the people at large. It also has roots in Marxism or in that general kind of socialism which circulated at the beginning of this century, as well as roots in the strengths and most noble elements of the American character. As it was characterized by its leading expo-nent and most outstanding figures through its greatest period in the 1950's and 1960's, the movement for black equality was a religiously stamped movement.

No one who heard Martin Luther King, Jr., preach could deny the very real roots of his thought in Biblical Christianity, with its concern for fellowman as brother, with its call for the treatment of all men with brotherly love, and with its gospel of a struggle for human dignity without hatred and—above all things—without violence. The Negroes in America were a people without a past, without a heritage except what they had forged for themselves out of the bits and pieces of what was left over to them as a subject and subjugated people, de-prived of everything. They were robbed even of their surnames and the knowledge of where their homelands were located. These people had pieced together with great toil and ingenuity a culture that immeasurably en-riched the larger American culture in music, art, poetry, and literature. But it was not an African culture as such. Rather, the Negro, of all the groups that inhabit these shores, became the most American, the most new of all

the new men here. One thing was granted the Negroes
by most of their masters, even in their days of serfdom—
the Bible and the teachings of Christianity. This great
tradition the Negro made his own, as it was his own,
according to the teachings of that Bible and the beliefs
of those who subscribed to it.

But there were other influences on the movement for
Negro equality (as well as on the other movements for
equality and justice that characterize twentieth-century
America). There was the movement that had its locus in
the generalized kind of socialist thinking, the democratic
Marxism, of Western Europe—the kind of socialized
thinking that influenced the labor movement and was
instrumental in bringing about in America the most
powerful labor movement on earth, which now unhap-
pily has become quite conservative. For the most part,
Communist thought and doctrine never spread among
the Negroes of America. Perhaps it was because they
were too much formed by the Biblical Christian image,
even when they were no better or worse in their living
than their white counterparts. Their culture was one of
the Book. Through the 1960's, the black civil rights
movement won many legal victories—so much so that in
the 1970's there are fewer black children attending segregated schools in the eleven states of the old Confederacy than there are in the border states or in the states
that were part of the Union. But, as I have pointed out
elsewhere, many of these legal victories were Pyrrhic
victories, for they were not followed by the acceptance,
toleration, and brotherhood that should have prevailed.
Residential segregation, the gentleman's agreement, the
continuing disdain for men of another color remain perhaps more incisively present in the North and in the
large cities than in the South and in the rural areas of our
country. Nevertheless, the legal and outward victories of

the black civil rights movement inspired other groups—groups that had a sense of identity and also felt themselves to be prevented from exercising full legal and human rights—to work now for an equality of opportunity and position. Among these groups were women. The rise of the women's liberation movement certainly struck mankind, in the male sense of that term, as a surprise. Of course, the movement for the franchise of women was a very old story, having been fought over in the nineteenth and early twentieth centuries. It too had its legal and Pyrrhic victory very early, with its amendment to the Constitution (the 19th Amendment, ratification certified August 26, 1920) giving women the right to vote.

Women's liberation came with a bang and is still with us, largely as a vast propaganda movement. In a short period of time it has won an immense number of victories. Now it is no longer possible to describe jobs in help-wanted advertisements as being for "men only." Women have certainly been subject to unfair treatment by the most "liberal" institutions. For example, it has been shown again and again how the universities, with their high claims to liberality, have underpaid and underpromoted women with the same credentials as men. A new awareness of the severe discrimination of the South came when, as a college student there, I learned that the State Department of Education in South Carolina had four separate schedules of payment: one for white men, one for white women, one for black men, and one for black women. The Department of Education there really had a clear vision of the order in which the world was to be arranged.

To the revolutionary tumult among American blacks struggling for justice and liberty, the demands of American Indians for admittance into the mainstream of American culture, and the starkly shrill demands of the women's liberation movement, we must add the revolution of middle-class youth. Having written extensively in *The New Mentality*[61] and in *A New Kind of Man*[62] about the movement of youth toward the establishment of a new, more humane culture, I will not develop this theme here. We must see that the various youth movements that swept over American college and university campuses and swept down to the level of the high school and junior high school in our larger cities formed part of a demand for a redress of grievances on the part of a subsection of the American citizenry.

We must, however, take note of a recent and very significant symbolic development in the efforts of the nation at least to consider redressing the grievances expressed by youth. This was the holding of the 1971 White House Conference on Youth at Estes Park, Colorado, in April, 1971. *The Report of the White House Conference on Youth*,[63] distributed widely to members of the "power structure," is full of evidence that young people are not guilty of the sin of criticizing the Establishment's policies without giving alternative suggestions. This censure of youthful critiques is often heard but is absolutely unjustified. What is the case is that the President and all of the members of the power structure simply refuse to heed the suggestions given them by young people. A reading of the 310-page report will show just how many suggestions were given. For example, the task force on foreign relations, in a majority report, states that it "rejects the Administration's continuing plea for a gradual withdrawal to be terminated at some unspecified date as one last attempt to influence militarily the eventual outcome of the war in Indo-China." It goes on to recommend total and immediate cessation of United States ground, naval, and bombing operations there.

Further, it "recommends total withdrawal of all U.S. military forces and cessation of logistical support, both overt and covert, from Indo-China by December 31, 1971."[64]

During the same conference the Indochina caucus proposed that the United States work for the admission of Cuba, North Korea, and North Vietnam, along with Red China, to the United Nations and that the United States grant them diplomatic recognition.

To show how willing young people are to give alternative suggestions and how unwilling older people are to accept them, we quote further from the report: "In view of the fact that the government has repeatedly lied to us; we recommend the White House Conference on Youth delegates demand the immediate resignation of President Nixon and Vice President Agnew and all their staff."[65] As of now this suggestion has not been acted upon.

An Old Man's Country

Looking at the House of Representatives and the Senate of the United States, we can see that what the women, the blacks, the Indians, and the youth tell us is true—that ours is a society dominated by old white men. This is hardly fair or sensible in a day when such a very large number of people are below the age of thirty in America, in a century when young men of eighteen have repeatedly been called upon to offer their lives in war without being given the franchise. But this has now been granted them. The Nixon Administration has championed and signed a bill giving eighteen-year-old youth the right to vote. Although we have not been able to tell what effect this will have upon the body politic, we can only hope that it will translate into voting action the oft-expressed youthful desires for a more human and a less mechanized, less economically exploitive society than has hitherto existed in America.

But in considering the problem of redressing grievances, we should also recall that there are groups that have not yet made their just demands. We can only wait in anticipation of the possible fatal consequences to the United States as a nation when these people do rise up with their claims to full participation. I mention here only two of the major groups: the white poor, urban and rural, spread throughout the fifty states, and the people of the region known as Appalachia, in the upper Southern and lower Northern states. The Appalachian poor have not received anything like the reward commensurate with the services they have rendered the nation. From their mountains have come timber, coal, and oil; from their numbers have come hundreds of thousands of volunteers for the Armed Forces; from them hundreds of thousands of people have come to the large Northern and Southern cities to serve in the industrial armies of the nation. Appalachia itself has been ravished and left to rot. This no longer can be tolerated. Both our rising sense of humaneness and justice and our rising belief that we are destroying the earth by our economic practices force us to look again at Appalachia and the Appalachian people.

A SOCIETY OF REALIZED EQUALITY

How will we achieve a society of realized equality? As yet no one knows. And yet the broad outlines of such a movement do lie ready to hand if we have the vision to see them and the courage to pick up these elements and develop them.

First, an automatic registration of voters—an automatic, computerized operation that would enter the names of living citizens upon the voter registration rolls in their district upon their attaining age eighteen—would have a great deal to do with spreading true equality in the United States. As it is now, even with the striking down of the poll tax and other tax considerations by an amendment to the Constitution, there are so many conflicting regulations, so much gerrymandering, so much arrogance and dishonesty in the administration of policies by local clerks of court and party registrars, that many people are deprived of the right to take part in the electoral process. Automatic registration to vote would overcome some of these difficulties.

Again, the residency requirements, which vary from state to state and from locality to locality, generally require six months of residency in a state and thirty days of residency in a precinct before one is entitled to vote. These ought to be abolished by federal law. In the United States, even as long as ten years ago, one family in every five moved once a year. This mobility is increasing rather than decreasing. This means that millions upon millions of American citizens are effectively disenfranchised by the archaic restrictions of our political apparatus. We have built a society in which mobility equals success, and many times mobility is the only possible way that one can maintain himself in a job to support his family. Why then should these archaic restrictions, based on conditions prevailing in an earlier period in our national life when the county seat was one day's journey from a man's farm, keep at least one fifth of the potential electorate from voting for president, governor, and the other representatives of their choice, just because they have to move?

Again, the society we have built here in the latter part of the twentieth century is one in which the ownership of real estate and property is not a desirable goal for millions of people. The very mobility mentioned above militates against real estate purchase. The growth of our population has meant that less and less land is available for people to purchase and settle upon. It is true that the poor and those who have been discriminated against in the job market also have great difficulty in acquiring properties. Therefore realized equality, at least in the political sense, would be greatly enhanced if all real estate or financial requirements or so-called responsibility requirements for voting would be disallowed in all portions of the United States.

Another measure that might help toward the realization of equality would be the institution of a plan similar to that introduced in Congress in 1971 by a number of senators and representatives. Such a plan would allow each taxpayer to check off a portion of his income tax payments to the Federal Government as a contribution to the presidential election expenses of the candidates of all major parties. I would suggest that each taxpayer be allowed to check off up to ten dollars of his paid taxes and be given the right to designate on his tax form, over his signature, the political party to which this tax money was to be paid.

A COUNTRY DEDICATED TO INTERNATIONAL COOPERATION

The issue of the possible passage of a general amnesty for draft dodgers and deserters from the Vietnam War has been raised by the remnant of the liberal establishment still in power in the United States. While such an amnesty would probably aid in reducing some of the ill feeling generated by the Vietnam conflict and the draft, no such measure seems desired by the young men who have been radicalized by the Southeast Asian adventure.

The movement for amnesty is seen by war resisters as an essentially liberal measure designed to make the middle-of-the-road liberal feel better. It is not really an answer to the radical critique of the direction in which American society has gone since 1947. However, if the Government did offer amnesty to the young men in Canada (where the majority of the war resisters are), it would make for better feelings on the part of some resisters and also between the Canadian government and the United States government. It would be an indication that the majority of the people in the United States wished to begin healing the wounds that have afflicted the American nation over the past decade.

Any amnesty issued would fail to satisfy the more radical resisters, to be sure. Such an amnesty would be accepted by some, and these persons could be offered the chance to further help heal the nation's social ills by working in governmental programs to attempt to overcome poverty and environmental pollution.

We cannot forget, in the future, the hundreds of thousands of young men who served in the Vietnam War. Congress has already passed some excellent legislation extending veterans benefits—including funds for education, training allowances, and guaranteed home loans—to this group of veterans. The only unfortunate thing that has developed so far seems to be the failure of a good many veterans to take advantage of these opportunities. These programs, like the program of the original G.I. Bill after World War II, are among the most efficient channels through which our society can be directed into more equalitarian forms. Since the vast majority of younger ex-servicemen come from the lower and lower-middle classes and might otherwise find it difficult to attend college, veterans benefits under the G.I. Bills are not only a reward for service but a form of social upgrading and a definite liberal movement toward equality. This social upgrading must be done again with the Vietnam veteran. Indeed, this period of service probably will produce, on a percentage basis, a greater number of black and other minority veterans than previous service periods did. By concentrating on educating the minority veteran to capitalize upon his veterans benefits great strides might be made toward breaking the cycle of poverty in rural depressed areas and in inner-city slums. This same kind of leverage can be attained, as it was attained after 1945, by the use of the "veterans preference" provision in filling civil service jobs. In fact, it might be a good idea to increase the margin of veterans preference beyond that now allowed. Perhaps a basic 10 percent bonus score could be given a veteran on civil service examinations plus a sliding number of points based on the length of his service and other factors such as the suffering of wounds and/or capture. This would be just and would also help in the employment of many veterans who might have difficulty with examinations.

The whole point of this is not to glorify the Vietnam War, but to help to compensate the person who had to bear the brunt of it, which was often as difficult psychologically, because of the polarization of the nation, as it was physically. We should take the opportunity as a society to attempt to overcome the alienation and bewilderment engrained in the Vietnam veteran by the events of the last decade and, insofar as it is the case that the relatively poor do most of the fighting in any war, to help the veteran upgrade his life. We need to remember the animosity in the Vietnam veteran—built up by the severe social struggle through which the United States is passing—just as much as we remember the hostility of the war resisters and the vocal criticism by the civilian opponents of the war. Until we overcome the polarization of the nation, we will not be able to dedicate our country to anything constructive.

The purpose of aiming the national will, through the achievement of a reasonable national consensus, toward international cooperation would be the securing of a viable state of peace in the world. This dedication to peace will necessitate a rather sharp change in the thinking of most governmental authorities, and, I dare say, of the majority of our population. It will be possible only if there is a downgrading of militarism in our society. Indeed, it will mean a return to the original principles on which the United States was built, principles that included a prohibition of the maintenance of large standing armies in time of peace. Rather, the only way the members of the "peace forces" in America, and citizens of other countries, will ever take seriously an American resolve to work for peace will be the implementation of the principles laid down in the Constitution and the Bill of Rights. Sometimes we forget that the grievances that brought about the American Revolution included the charge that the king kept large standing armies. We also forget that in our Bill of Rights the term "a well regulated militia" (which from the context is obviously a citizen army or reserve force) is mentioned rather than a permanent war machine.

A POSSIBLE TWO-PART MILITARY POLICY
FOR THE FUTURE

In regard to the above suggestion of a return by the United States to its original principles in military matters, the objection might be made that 1976 is not 1776. This is true, but the European nation of Switzerland, though surrounded by bellicose neighbors, has preserved its independence for centuries by a two-part military policy. I mention two parts because usually only one is developed in discussion. The first part of that policy is to keep Swiss hands out of the internal affairs of other states and not to attempt to sway world affairs by implicit or explicit saber-rattling. This is the part that most commentators overlook. The second part is to maintain a very large reserve army ready to come to the defense of the nation very quickly if anyone else attempts to interfere in the internal life of the Swiss. Given the resolution to fight as doggedly, once attacked, as they sought to keep out of conflict, Switzerland was able to coexist with neighbors as unlikely as Nazi Germany and Fascist Italy. Minding your business is perhaps the best defense in the complex modern world, and this by no means implies isolationism, since the Swiss are commercially and culturally active on a worldwide scale. Theirs is not a bad example.

It would be difficult for a country the size of the United States to move to the Swiss position immediately. But it could work toward such a two-part military policy. The present shrinkage of the Armed Forces could be accelerated. With withdrawal from Southeast Asia and the winding down of the draft, force levels could be cut drastically from the figure of between two and a half and three million men, which has been the average over the last twenty years, even outside of years of serious combat. Consideration might be given to economic incentives for men to join military reserve organizations. Something, at any rate, must be done with the reserve establishment, for it too will shrink with the disappearance of the draft and of the danger of active military service.

A number of factors are present in the real world of politics today that make a movement toward a more peaceful posture possible. These include the existence of the United Nations and its continuous service since 1945, despite the lack of real support and a number of real failures. The present political makeup of the United Nations, although not as advantageous to the United States as it has been in the past, may very well be a contributing plus to a more peaceful United States posture. By this I mean that the United States can no longer dictate the policies of the United Nations on major Cold War issues and obtain United Nations sanction for what it wanted to do anyway. That was the position of the United States and the United Nations in 1950. The addition of the mini-nations and of a considerable number of Third World states has made it impossible for the United States to dictate to the United Nations. Frankly, this is a more democratic position and one that can keep the United States out of trouble.

The recent moves of the Nixon Administration to improve the relations of the United States with Communist China and the Soviet Union are also signs of available resources for the creation of a realistic peace-seeking posture on our part. These relations must be pursued and deepened.

The round of SALT (Strategic Arms Limitation) talks concerning the control of nuclear weapons is also a plus factor for peace. No matter what the difficulties, such talks must be pursued, for the alternative is not only financial breakdown for the developed states in senseless arms races but the very real probability of a fatal blow to human civilization by a nuclear war.

The SALT talks must be expanded to include France and Communist China, however. It will do much less good for two or three of the nations that have nuclear weapons to come to an agreement if two other nuclear powers are not bound by the agreement. Perhaps the new cordiality between the United States and Communist China would make the entry of China into these talks more of a possibility. China has said that it would never be the first to use nuclear weapons in war. Again, in the case of France, the recent showing of the intention of being economically fair to France in the devaluation of the dollar might make France more willing to discuss serious attempts to limit its options with its presently independent nuclear strike force.

DEDICATION TO POLLUTION CONTROL

There will be no recovery of America worthy of the name if we do not truly start to recover the land, air, and water of the nation. The present widespread faddishness of concern for ecology must be deepened into a personal and national priority through the educational system. We must encourage government at every level to pass legislation that will eliminate all homeowner and industrial practices that now pollute the environment in ways that are subject to control. It is ridiculous for us to bury ourselves in our own garbage when the technological expertise that has brought us to this point can create systems of healthy disposal.

We must go beyond the elimination of polluting practices to the beginning of the recovery of all reversibly spoiled land, air, and water. We may do this right now by passing more restrictive legislation on strip mining and quarrying, and by an aggressive program designed to recover stripped areas. Reforestation—no new program—should be increased and extended. Perhaps the public school sytems could be enlisted to furnish young people for extensive tree-planting programs all over the country. The idealism of youth could be tapped in order to multiply the number of cleanup programs that are presently under way, sponsored by youth organizations.

Yet these essentially volunteer movements will remain too weak and scattered to accomplish much without massive federal legislation and money.

Federal legislative efforts might begin with the designation of more and more rivers as wilderness rivers and more and more undeveloped areas as public preserves. Certainly the Red River Gorge area of Kentucky should be protected from the ecocide threatened by the dams proposed to be built there. Other portions of the national territory that are relatively untouched must be preserved from further degrading, and the damage already done them must be reversed. Organizations in Appalachia such as Save Our Kentucky and leaders like Dr. Wayne Davis of the University of Kentucky and Dr. William Cohen of Hazard, Kentucky, ought to be supported by the government rather than harassed by the law, as is now the case. Every state now has such leaders and groups and they deserve individual, group, and governmental support.

The true leaders of the environmental awareness struggle have pointed out that everything turns upon the question of value. Value, unfortunately, in both the sciences and philosophy, has been an area of man's life that the twentieth century has deliberately overlooked. The positivistic attitude that has undergirded our assault on the fabric of the universe has assumed that values are no more than the desires that a man or group of men have wished to satisfy at any one time. To speak of a value or a set of values apart from some human desire that seeks gratification has been to court the charge of being unscientific or unphilosophical or both. The essence of the scientific approach has been to deny that value has the same ontological status as the movement of matter— which can be measured. The result has been a pragmatic, unsentimental approach to physical reality by men who either lacked an appreciative and respectful approach to the world or held a groundless, overly sentimentalized view of nature that lay alongside their scientific outlook and remained completely unassimilated by it—remained, in other words, as a surd. Such a schizophrenic, dualistic approach to the world means that one's handling of the earth is effectively divorced from a sense of values and even from long-term responsibility.

To skip the philosophic discussion and come straight to the point, man's unreasonable pollution of the earth is the direct result of his historically recent cult of efficiency in exploitation and maximization of profit, which is based on valueless reason. It is not the case that man has had no values, but rather that his values have been divorced from his science, his economics, and his overall philosophy. Man's reason, in the twentieth century, has been value-free and his values have been largely reason-free, or sentimental.

A sentimental man is one who can travel by car to the northern Michigan area to fish and enjoy the sun setting over Lake Michigan while his factory is pouring raw chemicals into the same lake near Chicago. Such a sentimental man enjoys the money he makes (by saving funds that could have been used to treat the raw chemicals). One day he notices that the fish are no longer around and may even curse the unthinking people who have spoiled his fishing. A sentimental man may be wealthy, may be educated, may be a sportsman, may be what our world calls a success, but a sentimental man is not reasonable.

The root of the problem of the misuse of the earth, from the perspective of the theologian, is the amoral conception that Western, civilized man has of the material elements of the world. Western man has also become quite amoral in his use and misuse of his fellowman, yet there are many just men who decry this situation and help to correct injustices from time to time. But, until recently, there were few men who would speak up for the nonhuman elements of the world—for animals, for the earth itself, for the forests, for the rivers and seas.

Today there is a growing number of people who are willing to stand up not only for the human elements but also for the nonhuman elements of the world. Many of these people are members of the scientific community, yet they are speaking out with very strong emotional feelings about man's responsibility to care for the whole earth—and this not just in scientific terms of pollution levels and the disappearance of wilderness areas. In effect, the first Earth Day, in April, 1970, was a kind of natural religious celebration for the now unsystematized but nevertheless real theology of the earth that is growing in intensity among sensitive people.

Man lives not only for knowledge but by knowledge. He lives not by values but for values. And only when man's knowledge and values are unified, enjoyed together in a serious and reverent whole, does he attain to wisdom.

It is such wisdom that we need now. We do not need a sentimentality about the world that lacks knowledge, for that will only deepen chaos. We do not need a positivistic knowledge without values, for that will only hasten ultimate destruction through exploitation. Wisdom is knowledge plus love. Wisdom is reverence toward a commitment to life plus knowledge of the facts about life. Only such wisdom can lead us to change our national attitudes and our national directions so that the beauty and healthfulness of the earth may be recovered, stabilized, and conserved.

It is becoming increasingly clear that the traditional

American position on freedom of the seas with an insistence on a twelve-mile limit for the extension of national sovereignty over bordering ocean areas simply does not fit the facts of the twentieth century. The claims of Peru and other nations to 200-mile-wide ocean borders make much more sense because of the ability such laws give governments to control pollution and over-exploitation of the marine environment and the coastal areas of their countries. The United States already has experienced depredations to its resources by offshore oil drilling in southern California and in the Gulf of Mexico. The threat to the East coast already exists in that it is now thought that there are large deposits of oil some 200 miles out in the Atlantic stretching from Maine to Virginia. The extension of the "territorial sea" to a 200-mile limit, only for the purpose of control of the exploitation of the marine environment and not for interference with the free use of the seas, would prevent unregulated foreign interests from exploiting these undersea resources and perhaps damaging the ecology of our Atlantic coast. This would be a case of nationalism in the interest of the protection of the planet. Certainly the laws against the polluting of the sea by oil drillers and by the shipment of oil in tankers should be made tougher and enforced more carefully.

A new look at American law regarding the territorial sea is also necessitated by the depletion of the offshore fisheries. Countries that maintain huge modern fishing fleets, such as Japan and the Soviet Union, are taking millions of tons of fish near the coast of United States territories in the North Atlantic and the North Pacific. An extension of territorial waters and a sterner enforcement of new laws designed to protect the very existence of many species of marine creatures would not be selfish national actions but actually responsible international actions. Not only fish but whales and seals need increased protection.

Although modern society needs more and more oil to operate its productive plant, consideration should be given to increasing the limitations upon offshore oil drilling. Along this same line, the exploitation of the North Slope of Alaska, with its proven oil reserves, should be severely regulated by federal laws and, if necessary, by the stationing of military forces in that area and along the route of any pipelines that may be built, to monitor environmental pollution.

CONFIDENCE IN LAW

No society can exist without law. Even the communards who have attempted to build Utopian communes in the last decade have discovered the need for rules and their enforcement whenever a group of people live together. There is nothing wrong with law, but something might be wrong with specific kinds of laws or with the way laws are enforced. In order to achieve sanity and stability in American society we must struggle to overcome the disrespect for law that has been generated by immature resistance to law, by law enforcement as such, and by the undemocratic and unethical enforcement of laws on the part of some policemen. Actions are legal or illegal depending upon whether they square with the law as it is written and interpreted by the courts, not upon whether they are done by civilians or police officials. The police (and here we mean only that minority of officers whose actions are similar to the activities pointed out as illegal by several presidential study commissions) must constantly be educated in the meaning of the law and the meaning of their responsibility to uphold the dignity of the law by just actions. At the same time, by way of the mass media and through the schools, the public must be educated in the need for law and the responsibility for each person to maintain laws that are drawn for the good of all citizens. Every schoolchild should have the opportunity to read the official report to the National Commission on the Causes and Prevention of Violence.[66] Also students in our schools and members of civic organizations and churches should study carefully the report by the President's Commission on Law Enforcement and the Administration of Justice[67] in order to see the complexity of the administration of justice in a society as large as ours.

So much has been written elsewhere about the increasing intrusion of governmental agencies upon the privacy of citizens that we will not say much here about this problem. Suffice it to say that the limits of what is constitutionally permissible and of what free people ought to have to endure have been transgressed any number of times by local, state, and federal police agencies and by intelligence units of the military itself. There has been systematic snooping in the affairs of private citizens and of elected officials such as congressmen and senators. The very thought of this being done by any agency of government without adequate cause is enough to chill the heart of any American. Such surveillance ought not to be carried on in the absence of some clear indication that such persons might be engaged in criminal activities, an indication so strong that warrants might be obtained from judges to authorize such investigations. Practices such as those exposed by a number of reporters and by members of Congress are typical of the police states established by the enemies of democracy such as the Nazis and the Stalinists. This situation must not be allowed to continue in this country. We will restore confidence in law enforcement more quickly by a severe restriction upon so-called "domestic intelligence" activities than by any other action.

In pointing out the excesses of governmental agencies and of the police, one does not gain favor in this country. But history will prove that the most loyal citizens are those who have been concerned enough about the right-wing drift of American society (well documented in both the report of the National Commission on the Causes and Prevention of Violence and the report of the President's Commission on Law Enforcement and the Administration of Justice) to bring out the facts so that the American people may be alerted. There is, of course, little personal advantage in so doing. Jean Jacques Rousseau pointed out that "speaking the truth is not the way to get ahead in the world; the people appoint no ambassadors, fill no chairs at universities, and confer no pensions."[68] Rousseau went on to observe that one of the prime causes for error in the will of the people is misinformation:

> The general will is always well-intentioned, i.e., . . . it always looks to the public good. It does not follow, however, that the people's deliberations are invariably and to the same extent what they ought to be. Men always will what is good for them, but do not always see what is good for them. The people is never corrupted, but is frequently misinformed. And only when it is misinformed does it give the appearance of willing what is bad for it.[69]

It would appear that there is a great deal of ignorance among the American people about what is allowable in a democratic society and about what is now taking place. The 1971 White House Conference on Youth was not ignorant, when its task force on legal rights and justice made the following recommendation to the President, which I would also recommend be implemented. Section 7.8 states:

> It is alleged that the Federal Bureau of Investigation has evolved into an overreaching (unwarranted) institution engaged in indiscriminate spying and surveillance activities on law-abiding and innocent citizens.
>
> Charges of improper and expanding activities leveled against the FBI have generated a chilling effect that has resulted in a feeling of fear and intimidation among the youth, minorities, and a significant number of people in this nation and members of both houses of the United States Congress.
>
> FBI investigations have smacked of political surveillance of citizens who express themselves by engaging in protesting public policies. Eavesdropping is not a legitimate function of the FBI where no crime or threat of crime or violence is involved.
>
> To counteract the excessive zeal of the FBI and other civilian intelligence agencies, we propose the creation of an Independent Review Board composed of Congressmen, judges, lawyers, intelligence officers, laymen, university professors, and youth, all of equal representation.
>
> The validity of all allegations leveled against the FBI is a question that needs to be answered by the Independent Review Board.
>
> The purpose of the Board would be to monitor all government agencies which gather intelligence information on civilians as well as national civilian agencies performing similar functions.
>
> The Board would issue an annual report and such other reports as deemed necessary and appropriate by its members. The Board should further be charged with recommending limitations on the scope of domestic intelligence by the FBI and other government and national civilian agencies.

In line with the above avowed purposes, said recommendations put forward by the Board should be reflected in support legislation. This legislation would include limitations on: (1) secret surveillance; (2) the maintenance of secret files; and (3) the use and accessibility of such secret files.

It is to be pointed out that the proper vehicle for such investigations as the proposed Board would undertake is not the Senate Constitutional Rights Subcommittee. This subcommittee has little rapport with the Justice Department, which itself has constantly balked at undertaking such investigations.[70]

Some such legislation and control upon governmental activity is needed if we are to have the kind of America we want in the future.

PUBLIC SANITY AN ANSWER TO DRUGS

In the last analysis, the most complex of the issues underlying the rise of drug abuse in America is a sense of the feeling of estrangement from our government and from the direction in which our nation is moving. If the other kinds of problems discussed in this book are dealt with constructively—if peace is obtained in Southeast Asia, if we do give national priority to the struggles against poverty and ignorance and disease, if we do turn our attention to the salvation of the environment—we may inspire our young people to commit themselves to long-term constructive efforts that will preclude their becoming lost in the maze of drug abuse. Certainly, to help overcome youth's alienation, which is now often justified, would be a step toward the control of the drive to seek any other state of consciousness but the public one. I am saying that when we return to some form of sanity in our public life, the state of sane consciousness will not seem such a drag, and the lure of inner worlds will not be so great.

REFORMING EDUCATION

Finally, America must reform its educational efforts from the kindergarten through the doctoral program of its universities. This is not a question of more and more money and more and more people but, I think, of future progress by subtraction. Education will be reformed by severely reducing the amount of funds granted universities by the state and federal governments and by eliminating many of the third- and fourth-class universities that now exist. We should pour more money into pre-school education and early care of our children and into the grade schools and high schools rather than into the great devouring maw of higher education. We should also work to achieve alternative paths to adult recognition beyond the route of graduation from a university. The young people on the President's commission, which prepared the youth report, were aware of this problem. They said:

> Historically, America has placed blind faith in education. Our educational system has partially at least served us well.
>
> There is mounting evidence, however, that public confidence in education is eroding and that the whole system should undergo a thorough review.
>
> The greatest deficiency in American education is the absence of a clear cut organizing principle, a conceptually simple reason for being. The time has come to correct this debilitating deficiency.
>
> The Task Force on Education for the White House Conference on Youth, therefore, proposes the following which should serve as philosophic guidelines for educational

leadership in the 1970's and beyond. Educational leadership and educators should be held accountable for implementing this policy.

(1) Our ultimate concern is with the human spirit and human minds and not schools. In short we should concern ourselves with human fulfillment. Schools are not ends within themselves but rather vehicles through which "the young and old unite in the imaginative consideration of learning."

(2) Within the realm of potential of every human being there is a level of awareness and achievement which can make life rewarding. Most people want desperately to find that level.

(3) It is the responsibility of educational leadership to devise programs which reach out to the student and engage him in a process which is both interesting and fair and will, thus, lead to a level of awareness and achievement which gives him a positive perception of himself and his relationship to others.

(4) Any subject can be taught in an intellectually honest and interesting way by the competent, imaginative teacher who cares, given the necessary resources.[71]

Farther along the young people said:

What sense does it make to educate the young to love freedom and respect different ideas and ways of life, to work hard for social justice, if suddenly they will be involved in a war or a crisis provoked either by a quest for power or for economic hegemony or, tragically enough, because of a very distorted view of the world and the role of their nation in it?[72]

They went on to ask:

What sense does it make to learn science, if it is going to be applied in the systematic killing and repression of the people of the world?

What sense does it make to develop a skill that will fulfill one's life, if one day a nuclear war gets started and we all end losers, but no one left to state it?

What sense does it make to educate paranoid people?[73]

They then made the following recommendations:

(1) People should be educated to be free, to live harmoniously in a society where they can fulfill their potentialities, to respect the rights of others on a basis of justice, peace and love.

(2) The next generation needs to be educated with an intense, realistic awareness of the situation of the world, and to where this world is heading. It should be prepared in the educational process to accept a more broad and functional definition of humanity other than a conglomerate of nations in a permanent display of conflict of interests, wars and chaos. . . .

(3) Governments and media should stop the systematic propagandistic education, information and entertainment, dealing with nations and peoples with different ways of life. These distort reality, create fanaticism and fantasies, undermine the mentality and values of a free country, and induce totalitarianism.

(4) The education of the people should be in consonance with the main stream of principles and assumptions, upon which the actions of the different branches of government are based and justified. In the long run, it is not possible to educate people to believe in things which are opposite to those their governments believe, to behave contrary to their conscience on behalf of the demands of their social system. Governments should stop killing in the name of anything, to exploit in the name of development, to be corrupt and impose themselves in the name of national security. People should be educated to detest wars, not to glorify them; and to detest exploitation, not to perpetuate it by accepting it.[74]

ALTERNATIVE EDUCATIONS

Many organizations and committees have called for alternative routes to education in America. What possibilities are there for alternatives to the college career, other than to institute mimicries of the college education off campus?

We could reestablish the old apprenticeship system in many fields. Why couldn't one learn to be a lawyer by being an apprentice or a clerk to a lawyer? Many great jurists had their education in precisely this way. Why, too, could not a great deal of modern medical skills be imparted to apprentice medical students? After all, a large amount of medicine is not book memorization or investigation in a laboratory, but the learning of practical affairs in hospitals and things that can be gained only by an internship. Medical colleges could be reduced in size and number if the younger students were farmed out among doctors who could teach them on the job. The basic medical courses could be taken in present departments of biological sciences at state universities. Incidentally, this might help to increase the level and the possibility of medical care in many places in the United States. The same holds true for dentistry, where much could be learned by an apprenticeship to an older dentist. Certainly this could hold true for the ministry. Other than historical books, doctrinal books, and philosophy, most of what the minister needs to study in preparation for parish work could be learned in an internship, on the job, serving a church under an older minister. This was the case for a long time until the seminaries as we know them today were established. It could be done again. Again, it might be a way of serving people in the church better than we are now able to do.

Upgrading the community college system would also

be a good move. The community college's existence means that many persons might have an opportunity to go to college who otherwise would not. It also means that the state could educate without building more useless and costly dormitories. If anything has been the cause of the destruction of university morale and finances, it has been the building of great numbers of large dormitories. Is the university in the business of education or is it there to provide hotel space? Most of the problems with students, it would seem to me, arise from the living and eating arrangements as well as from the university's governance of their lives in dormitories. If, like Europe, we did not provide dormitories but treated college people as grownups and let them find their own shelter, we would have far fewer problems. Fortunately, the community college can escape this kind of danger.

THE RECOVERY OF AMERICA

Finally, we must stop to ask, What is the theological significance of each of these areas discussed? It seems to me that there is one brief answer that covers every problematic area mentioned in this book. That answer is itself a question: Looking at tomorrow, standing in the present, recognizing our problems, shall we as thinking people continue to be ministers of injustice or will we try now to become healers of long-standing ills?

I do not see how any religious man, or any serious man of no religion, can give any other answer to that question than this: Let the future use me, in whatever new and dangerous way it will, to heal the wounds of my people.

NOTES

1. Bill Moyers, *Listening to America* (Harper's Magazine Press, 1971).

2. John Steinbeck, *Travels with Charley: In Search of America* (The Viking Press, Inc., 1962).

3. Bernard Fall, *Last Reflections on a War* (Doubleday & Company, Inc., 1967).

4. The young Ohio girl was Vickie Cole, daughter of the Rev. David Cole, pastor of the United Methodist Church in Deshler, Ohio.

5. The 1970 figure is from *Britannica Book of the Year, 1972* (Encyclopaedia Britannica, 1972), p. 629. See also Michael Harrington, *The Other America: Poverty in the United States* (Penguin Books, Inc., 1962), and Jack E. Weller, *Yesterday's People: Life in Contemporary Appalachia* (University of Kentucky Press, 1965).

6. These figures reflect the situation of withdrawal from Vietnam as of the beginning of 1972.

7. *The Pentagon Papers*, with commentary by Neil Sheehan (Bantam Books, Inc., 1971).

8. Banning Garrett, "Cambodia Takes Up the Gun," *Ramparts*, Vol. IX, No. 2 (Aug., 1970), pp. 32–53; Roger Williams, "Pacification in Viet-Nam," *Ramparts*, Vol. VII, No. 12 (May, 1969), pp. 21–24; and Frank Browning and Banning Garrett, "The New Opium War," *Ramparts*, Vol. IX, No. 10 (May, 1971), pp. 32 ff.

9. See Charles A. Reich, *The Greening of America: The Coming of a New Consciousness and the Rebirth of a Future*

(Random House, Inc., 1970). Also see Philip Nobile, *The Con III Controversy* (Pocket Books, Inc., 1971).

10. John Charles Cooper, *The Turn Right* (The Westminster Press, 1970).

11. *Encyclopaedia Britannica*, 14th ed., s.v. "Indian, North American."

12. See *Encyclopaedia Britannica*, 14th ed., "Declaration of Independence."

13. The reproduction of life on the Eastern seaboard farther and farther west is essentially what happened. Note the occurrence over and over of town names from Maryland, Pennsylvania, and Virginia, in Ohio, Kentucky, Indiana, and Illinois (for example: Richmond, Virginia; Richmond, Kentucky; Richmond, Indiana; and even Richmond, California).

14. See Dee Alexander Brown, *Bury My Heart at Wounded Knee: An Indian History of the American West* (Holt, Rinehart & Winston, Inc., 1971). Also see Chief Red Fox, *The Memoirs of Chief Red Fox*, ed. by Cash Asher (McGraw-Hill Book Co., Inc., 1971).

15. See the novels of John Steinbeck—for example, *The Grapes of Wrath* (Bantam Books, Inc., 1970).

16. From *The Spirit of American Philosophy*, ed. by Gerald E. Myers (G. P. Putnam's Sons, Inc., 1970), pp. 91–92.

17. See my discussion of the covenants of society in *The Turn Right*, pp. 158–162.

18. See *Republic or Empire? The Philippine Question*, by William Jennings Bryan *et al.* (Chicago: The Independence Co., 1899).

19. In 1971, President Nixon's administration turned over the Swan Islands, "guano islands" in the Caribbean Sea, to Honduras. The United States annexed the Swan Islands in 1863. Honduras claimed them from 1923 onward.

20. C. L. R. James, "Colonialism and National Liberation in Africa: The Gold Coast Revolution," in *National Liberation*, ed. by Norman Miller and Roderick Aya (The Free Press, 1971), pp. 102–136.

21. *Ibid.*, pp. 103–104.

22. See Frantz Fanon, *The Wretched of the Earth* (Grove Press, Inc., 1968).

23. See "The Land Question and Black Liberation," in Eldridge Cleaver, *Post-Prison Writing and Speeches* (A Ramparts Book, Random House, Inc., 1969), pp. 57–79. Also see Roderick Aya and Norman Miller (eds.), *The New American Revolution* (The Free Press, 1971).

24. Cleaver, *op. cit.*, pp. 78–79.

25. See H. J. Eysenck, *The IQ Argument: Race, Intelligence and Education* (The Library Press, 1971). See *The Humanist*, Vol. XXXII, No. 1 (Jan.–Feb., 1972), for a full issue devoted to "I.Q. and Race." The following sources may be used for further information:

a. *Environment, Heredity, and Intelligence*. Compiled from *Harvard Educational Review*. Reprint Series No. 2. *Harvard Educational Review*, 1969. This volume includes papers by A. Jensen.

b. *The IQ Argument: Race, Intelligence and Education*, by H. J. Eysenck. The Library Press, 1971.

c. *"I.Q.,"* by Richard Herrnstein. *Atlantic*, Vol. 228, No. 3 (Sept., 1971), pp. 44–64.

d. "Unknowns in the IQ Equation," a review of the above three writings, by Sandra Scarr-Salapatek. *Science*, Vol. 174, Dec. 17, 1971, pp. 1223–1228.

e. "IQ and Race," an ethical forum with articles by A. Jensen, J. Kagan, D. McClelland, R. Light, H. Eysenck, W. Shockley, and K. Clark. *The Humanist*, Jan.–Feb., 1972.

26. See Cooper, *The Turn Right*.

27. See Rudolf Bultmann *et al.*, *Kerygma and Myth*, ed. by H. W. Bartsch (Harper Torchbooks, Harper & Row, Publishers, Inc., 1961).

28. See *The Journal of the American Academy of Religion*, Vol. XXXIX, No. 3 (Sept., 1971), for a discussion of myth by Stephen Crites, "The Narrative Quality of Experience."

29. See John Charles Cooper, *The New Mentality* (The Westminster Press, 1969).

30. Sydney J. Harris in the *Chicago Daily News*, June 22, 1971.

31. See LeRoy Moore, Jr., "From Profane to Sacred America: Religion and the Cultural Revolution in the United States," *The Journal of the American Academy of Religion,* Vol. XXXIX, No. 3 (Sept., 1971), pp. 321–338.

32. *Ibid.*

33. See Burrhus Frederic Skinner, *Beyond Freedom and Dignity* (Alfred A. Knopf, Inc., 1971); also see his article of the same title in *Psychology Today,* Vol. V, No. 3 (Aug., 1971), pp. 31–81.

34. See Viktor Frankl, *Man's Search for Meaning: An Introduction to Logotherapy* (a newly revised and enlarged edition of *From Death-Camp to Existentialism*), tr. by Ilse Lasch (Beacon Press, Inc., 1963).

35. *Psychology Today,* Vol. V, No. 3 (Aug., 1971), pp. 31–81.

36. Gordon G. Gallup, Jr., "Chimps and Self-Concept—It's Done with Mirrors," *Psychology Today,* Vol. IV, No. 10 (Mar., 1971), pp. 58 ff.; and Dian Fossey, "Making Friends with Mountain Gorillas," *National Geographic,* Vol. 137, No. 1 (Jan., 1970), pp. 48–67.

37. See Christopher Jencks and David Riesman, *The Academic Revolution* (Doubleday & Company, Inc., 1968).

38. See G. William Domhoff, *Who Rules America?* (Prentice-Hall, Inc., 1967); C. Wright Mills, *The Power Elite* (Galaxy Books, 1959); and C. Wright Mills, *Power, Politics and People,* ed. by Irving L. Horowitz (Ballantine Books, Inc., 1963).

39. See Note 5.

40. See Thomas Luckmann, *The Invisible Religion: The Problem of Religion in Modern Society* (The Macmillan Company, 1967).

41. Johannes Pedersen, *Israel: Its Life and Culture* (London: Oxford University Press, 1959).

42. Cooper, *The Turn Right.*

43. Editors of *Ebony* magazine, *The Black Revolution* (Johnson Publications, 1970).

44. Richard D. Knudten (ed.), *Criminological Controversies* (Appleton-Century-Crofts, 1968), pp. 13–20.

45. Cooper, *The Turn Right,* pp. 157–158.

46. Information from *The Toledo Blade,* Jan. 13, 1972, p. 16.

47. *Britannica Book of the Year, 1971* (Encyclopaedia Britannica, 1971), p. 300.

48. *Ibid.,* States Statistical Supplement, p. 42.

49. *Ibid.,* States Statistical Supplement, p. 41.

50. See Alvin Toffler, *Future Shock* (Random House, Inc., 1970).

51. Luis Marden, "Titicaca, Abode of the Sun," *National Geographic,* Vol. 139, No. 2 (Feb., 1971), pp. 272–294.

52. See John Charles Cooper, *A New Kind of Man* (The Westminster Press, 1972), pp. 110–112.

53. Robert Perske, "The Theological Views of Some of My Mentally Retarded Friends," *Pastoral Psychology,* Vol. XXII, No. 219, pp. 45–48.

54. See "The Unfinished Business of America" in *Look* magazine, July 12, 1971, p. 57.

55. *Ibid.,* p. 61.

56. *Ibid.,* p. 62.

57. *Ibid.*

58. Toffler, *op. cit.*

59. *Ibid.,* p. 15.

60. *Ibid.*

61. Cooper, *The New Mentality.*

62. Cooper, *A New Kind of Man.*

63. *The Report of the White House Conference on Youth,* April 18–22, 1971, Estes Park, Colorado (U.S. Government Printing Office, 1971).

64. *Ibid.,* p. 142.

65. *Ibid.,* p. 274.

66. See the official report to the National Commission on the Causes and Prevention of Violence, published as *Rights in Conflict,* ed. by Daniel Walker (A Signet Broadside, New American Library, Inc., 1968).

67. See the report by the President's Commission on Law Enforcement and the Administration of Justice, published as

The Challenge of Crime in a Free Society (Avon Books, 1968).

68. Jean Jacques Rousseau, *The Social Contract*, tr. and with an introduction by Willmoore Kendall (Gateway Edition, Henry Regnery Company, 1954), p. 38.

69. *Ibid.*

70. *The Report of the White House Conference on Youth,* 1971, pp. 170–171.

71. *Ibid.*, pp. 100–101.

72. *Ibid.*, p. 103.

73. *Ibid.*

74. *Ibid.*, pp. 103–104.